Nietzsche's *Genealogy of Morality*

Nietzsche's *Genealogy of Morality*

David Owen

McGill-Queen's University Press
Montreal & Kingston • Ithaca

ISBN: 978-0-7735-3348-6 (bound)
ISBN: 978-0-7735-3349-3 (paper)

Legal deposit third quarter 2007
Bibliothèque nationale du Québec

Published in 2007 simultaneously in the United Kingdom by Acumen Publishing
Limited and in North America by McGill-Queen's University Press

Library and Archives Canada Cataloguing in Publication

Owen, David, 1964-
    Nietzsche's Genealogy of morals / David Owen.

Includes bibliographical references and index.
ISBN 978-0-7735-3348-6 (bound)
ISBN 978-0-7735-3349-3 (pbk.)

    1. Nietzsche, Friedrich Wilhelm, 1844-1900. Zur Genealogie der
Moral. I. Title.

    B3313..Z73O94 2007   170   C2007-902153-0

Designed and typeset by Kate Williams, Swansea.
Printed and bound by Cromwell Press, Trowbridge.

For Caroline

Contents

Acknowledgements

The initial spur to write this study was my teaching a course on the idea of genealogy in Nietzsche and Foucault while a German Academic Exchange Service (DAAD) Visiting Professor at the J. W. Goethe University in Frankfurt in 2000. I am grateful to the DAAD for making this possible. I am also much indebted to Peter Niesen for the original idea that I go to Frankfurt and for facilitating the process, as well as for his friendship over many years. The Faculty of Social and Political Sciences was a hospitable environment and particular thanks are due to Josef Esser, Ingeborg Maus and Hans-Jürgen Puhle. My stay was also greatly enhanced by the generosity of Axel Honneth as well as the puckish humour and analytical sharpness of Rainer Forst. I owe particular thanks to Martin Saar, who not only participated in my course on genealogy while writing his own doctoral thesis on Nietzsche and Foucault, but in doing so pushed me hard to clarify and, indeed, revise my understanding of their works. That this sojourn was quite as enjoyable as it was also owed much to the presence of, and late night bar discussions with, two other visitors: Bert van den Brink (Utrecht University) and Morten Raffnsoe-Moller (Aarhus University). It would be remiss not to also mention the cheerful mayhem that is the annual Frankfurt Kantians versus Hegelians football match, much of the energy of which was directed to the philosophical issue of whether a Nietzschean should play on the Kantian or Hegelian team (for the record, the answer turned out to be the Hegelian team – the final score of the match remains contested).

A first draft of the book was completed with the aid of an Arts and Humanities Research Board (AHRB) *Matching Research Leave* Fellowship for Spring 2003–Spring 2004. That draft has been through a number of revisions since on the basis of comments by Bert van den Brink, Chris Janaway, Peter Niesen, Paul Patton, Robert Pippin, Tracy Strong and James Tully, who all gave generously of their time to help improve my initial arguments (even though they may still disagree with some, perhaps much, of what remains). Chris, Paul, Robert and Tracy all also gave me access to (then) unpublished work of their own on matters relating to the *Genealogy*, which saved me from a number of errors. Bert and Jim kept me from becoming entirely Nietzsche-dominated by pressing me to draw out and develop the implications of my arguments for other projects. I owe a particular debt to Dan Conway, who sent me his own manuscript on the *Genealogy*, and I have certainly gained from reading Dan's rather different account as well as his comments on mine. I am also grateful to audiences in Aarhus, Berkeley, Cambridge, Durham, Frankfurt, Illinois, Nijmegen, Oxford, Southampton and Utrecht for comments on various papers that have contributed to the arguments of this book.

Throughout this process, my major intellectual debt has been – and is – to Aaron Ridley. Over the past decade and more, conversations with Aaron have been the major intellectual locus for my philosophical engagement with Nietzsche (and much else besides) and the existence of this book as it is would have been impossible without his friendship. He is, to repay a compliment, the virtual co-author of this book. Acknowledgment is due also to *The Avenue Bar* and *The Crown Inn* in Southampton, where the vast majority of these conversations took place. More particular thanks are due to the landlord, staff and regulars at *The King Alfred* in Winchester, in which much of this work was written, whose cheerful toleration for the eccentric in the corner was a necessary antidote to the inevitable moments of authorial nihilism. I am also grateful to Steven Gerrard and Tristan Palmer for their faith in this project and their cheerful responses to possibly inane queries on my part. Two initially anonymous reviewers for Acumen made a number of helpful suggestions and I am grateful to Keith Ansell-Pearson and Christa Davis Acampora for the time and care that they devoted to this task.

It remains for me to thank my wife, Caroline Wintersgill, to whom this work is dedicated. Her love takes many forms, not least a willingness to wield a red pen over my work. Completion of the first draft of this book was happily interrupted by the birth of our daughter Miranda and its final draft follows the birth of our son Arthur, both of whom have already demonstrated a lively commitment to the digestibility of Nietzsche's philosophy.

David Owen, Southampton 2007

Abbreviations and note on translations used in the text

In choice of translations I have generally favoured the edition of Nietzsche's works that is being produced under the aegis of Cambridge Texts in the History of Philosophy for its combination of quality and consistency of translation. Where texts had not yet appeared at the time of writing, as in the case of the edition of *Nietzsche's Later Writings* by my colleague Aaron Ridley, I have used what I take to be the best available alternative (although this was a difficult choice between the Oxford and Hackett editions for *Twilight of the Idols*, the latter having Tracy Strong's excellent introduction). The one major exception to this rule is the edition of the *Genealogy* itself and this may be worth some comment.

There are five easily available English editions of Nietzsche's *Genealogy*, of which four could be happily used in conjunction with this book. The exception is the (admittedly very cheap) Dover edition entitled *The Genealogy of Morals*, which reproduces H. B. Samuel's 1913 translation of the text. The remaining four are:

- *On the Genealogy of Morals*, Walter Kaufmann (ed.), Reg Hollingdale & Walter Kaufmann (trans.) (London: Random House, 1967).
- *On the Genealogy of Morality*, Keith Ansell-Pearson (ed.), Carol Diethe (trans.) (Cambridge: Cambridge University Press, 1994).
- *On the Genealogy of Morality*, Maudemarie Clark (ed.), Maudemarie Clark & Alan J. Swenson (trans.) (Indianapolis, IN: Hackett, 1998).
- *On the Genealogy of Morals*, Douglas Smith (ed. & trans.) (Oxford: Oxford University Press, 1998).

Each of these editions has its strengths. The Kaufmann edition has the wonderful flow that one associates with Reg Hollingdale's translations of Nietzsche but the introduction is now rather dated. The Ansell-Pearson edition very usefully includes all the passages from his earlier work that Nietzsche cites or refers to in the *Genealogy* but the introduction is not strong and there are a number of problems of translation. The Clark edition has easily the best introduction and the strongest scholarly apparatus, and the translation is fine but, to my ear, a little "academic" at times. The Smith edition is, in my view, the best overall translation and hence it is the one that I have used, although I do not find the introduction to be very helpful. (I should also note here that a second edition of the Ansell-Pearson edition for Cambridge University Press will appear shortly with a much improved translation and a revised introduction). The Hackett edition is, I think, currently the best overall edition for students but any of these four editions can reasonably be recommended.

A   *The Antichrist*, R. J. Hollingdale (trans.) (Harmondsworth: Penguin, 1968).

BGE   *Beyond Good and Evil*, R.-P. Horstmann & J. Norman (eds) (Cambridge: Cambridge University Press, 2002).

D   *Daybreak*, M. Clark & B. Leiter (eds) (Cambridge: Cambridge University Press, 1997).

EH   *Ecce Homo*, W. Kaufmann (trans.), in *On the Genealogy of Morals and Ecce Homo*, W. Kaufmann (ed.) (New York: Vintage Books, 1969).

GM   *On the Genealogy of Morals*, D. Smith (trans.) (Oxford: Oxford University Press, 1998).

GS   *The Gay Science*, B. Williams (ed.) (Cambridge: Cambridge University Press, 2001).

HAH   "Human, All Too Human", *Human, All Too Human*, vol. 1, E. Heller (ed.) (Cambridge: Cambridge University Press, 1986).

TI   *Twilight of the Idols*, D. Large (trans.) (Oxford: Oxford University Press, 1998).

UM   *Untimely Meditations*, D. Breazeale (ed.) (Cambridge: Cambridge University Press, 1997).

WS   "The Wanderer and his Shadow", *Human, All Too Human*, vol. 2, E. Heller (ed.) (Cambridge: Cambridge University Press, 1986).

Introduction

Nietzsche's polemical text *On the Genealogy of Morality* is a brilliantly incisive attack on European "morality" that poses a disquieting challenge to the presumed value of our moral values. Combining philosophical acumen with psychological insight in prose of remarkable rhetorical power, Nietzsche takes up the task of offering us reasons to engage in a re-evaluation of our values. Yet if this is Nietzsche's project, as most commentators agree, we are confronted with a puzzle that has been succinctly stated by Philippa Foot: "Why do so many contemporary moral philosophers, particularly of the Anglo-American analytic school, ignore Nietzsche's attack on morality and just go on as if this extraordinary event in the history of thought had never occurred?" (1994: 3). With the notable exceptions of Bernard Williams, who broadly shared Nietzsche's suspicions (see in particular Williams 1993; also Clark 2001), and Foot herself, who attempts to respond to Nietzsche's attack (albeit on the mistaken grounds that Nietzsche is committed to the priority of aesthetic over moral values),[1] it seems that twentieth-century analytic moral philosophy has preferred to ignore rather than address the challenge that Nietzsche poses. In contrast, in what has become known (slightly misleadingly) as "continental philosophy", Nietzsche has consistently been acknowledged as a central figure of modern philosophy. Indeed Gilles Deleuze claims "It is clear modern philosophy has largely lived off Nietzsche" (1983: 1). Whatever one makes of this remark, it is clear that there is a sharp distinction between Nietzsche's reception within "analytic" and "continental" camps and it is hard not to share Foot's sense that the lack of engagement of analytic philosophy should puzzle us, representing as it does something of a failure of philosophical responsibility on the part of this tradition.

1

Yet if Nietzsche's challenge remains largely unaddressed by analytic philosophy, this may also be, in part, because the character of this challenge, the range of arguments deployed in articulating it and the reasons governing the particular rhetorical form taken by these arguments has not itself been adequately elucidated.[2] To attempt to set out, as clearly as possible, the nature of this challenge is the task of this enquiry. More precisely, my aim is to do four things:

- to offer an account of how Nietzsche comes to the project of the re-evaluation of values;
- to show how the development of his understanding of the requirements of this project leads him to acknowledge the need for the kind of investigation of "morality" that he will term "genealogy";
- to elucidate the general structure and substantive arguments of *On the Genealogy of Morality*, accounting for the rhetorical form of these arguments;
- to debate the character of genealogy (as exemplified by Nietzsche's *Genealogy*) as a form of critical enquiry.

I shall lay out the relationship of these tasks to the structure of the analysis of Nietzsche's project offered in this book in §II below; however, it may be worth prefacing this structural guide to my enquiry by offering some brief remarks on Nietzsche and the history of moral philosophy.

I

Nietzsche's relationship to the history of moral philosophy can be engaged in a number of ways; thus, one could stress his commitment to a naturalistic account of ethics and, hence, his connection to a philosophical trajectory that would encompass Aristotle, Spinoza and Hume, or one might emphasize his commitment to an account of the binding character of ethical commitments in terms of autonomy and, hence, his engagement with Kant and Hegel, to mention but two possible options. But the most crucial dimension of Nietzsche's relationship to the history of moral philosophy is his critical role as a philosophical innovator who introduces a new question into the field of moral philosophy: what is the value of our moral values? And hence also a new project: the re-evaluation of moral values. This is not to say that Nietzsche is the first to engage in a project of re-evaluation since Nietzsche himself regards the displacement of classical ethics by Christian ethics as a process of re-evaluation (one that he will seek to account for in his *Genealogy*) and one might reasonably argue that Machiavelli had engaged in a project of the re-evaluation of political values, Hume in the re-evaluation of religious values and perhaps even Bentham in the re-evaluation of governmental values. However, in raising the question of the value of our European Judeo-Christian moral values, the value of "morality", Nietzsche attempts to force an awareness of the salience of this question and, hence, of the project of the re-evaluation of moral values into the consciousness of moral philosophy.

Nietzsche's motivation for raising and pressing this question is driven to a significant degree by his sense that both the character of European ethical culture and the character of modern moral philosophy have been shaped by our Christian inheritance and that this inheritance has now been discredited:

> To view nature as if it were proof of the goodness and protection of God; to interpret history to the honour of a divine reason, as continual witness to a moral world-order and its ultimate moral intentions; to explain one's own experiences, as pious peoples have for long enough explained them, as if everything were predetermined, everything a sign, everything designed to promote the redemption of the soul: that time is *past*, it has conscience *against* it, it seems to all finer consciences, indecent, dishonest, deceitful, feminism, weakness, cowardice – in this rigour, if in anything, we are *good Europeans* and heirs to Europe's longest and boldest process of self-overcoming.   (GS §357; also cited in GM III §27)

In this passage, Nietzsche sums up the starting-point of his philosophical project: belief in God, in Providence, in redemption of the (immortal) soul is *discredited*. "What is now decisive against Christianity is our taste, no longer our reasons" (GS §132). After Bayle, Hume, Kant, Schopenhauer and Darwin, further philosophical criticism of such beliefs from an epistemic standpoint is superfluous. This, however, is a *starting*-point for Nietzsche because he takes the consequences of "the death of God" to cut deeper than European philosophy and, indeed, European culture is yet willing or, perhaps, able to acknowledge. Indeed, if Nietzsche has a claim to be the most important of modern moral philosophers, the grounds of this claim lie, first and foremost, in his recognition that the philosophical and cultural consequences of the death of God extend into the fabric of our lives with implications for the viability and value of the evaluative orientations that guide and display our modern forms of living. With regard to European culture, Nietzsche is thus raising the issue of how, now, we are to orient ourselves ethically; in respect of moral philosophy, he is prompting the question of how moral philosophy can responsibly address the issue of our ethical orientation. Nietzsche's proposal is that we experimentally call into question the value of "morality".

It is against this background that Nietzsche wonders in Book V of *The Gay Science*, with what I take to be a sense of genuine perplexity, why he has not encountered philosophers who approach "morality" as a problem and then comments:

> It is evident that up to now morality was no problem at all but, on the contrary, precisely that on which after all mistrust, discord, and contradiction one could agree – the hallowed place of peace where our thinkers took a rest even from themselves, took a deep breath and felt revived. I see nobody who ventured a *critique* of moral valuations; I miss even the slightest attempts of scientific curiosity, of the refined, experimental imagination of psychologists and historians that readily anticipates a problem and catches it in flight without quite knowing what it has caught. (GS §345)

He had made a related point earlier in *Beyond Good and Evil*, arguing that modern European philosophy has become fixated on the task of grounding "morality"; modern philosophers, he writes, "wanted morality to be *grounded*, – and every philosopher so far has thought that he has provided a ground for morality" (BGE §186). As Nietzsche points out, this implies that they took the value and character of morality itself as a given:

> As strange as it may sound, the problem of morality itself has been *missing* from every "science of morals" so far: there was no suspicion that anything was really a problem. Viewed properly, the "grounding of morals" (as philosophers called it, as they demanded it of themselves) was only an erudite form of good *faith* in the dominant morality, a new way of *expressing* it; as such, it was itself already situated within the

4

terms of a certain morality. In the last analysis, it even constitutes a type of denial that these morals *can* be regarded as a
problem.   (*Ibid.*)

Nietzsche's own example is provided by Schopenhauer; however, this
point can be usefully illustrated by the case of Kant. Consider that
Kant's *Groundwork of the Metaphysics of Morals*, as Hill points out,
"takes the data of moral intuitions as authoritative and tests Kant's
moral theory against them" (2003: 196) before turning to provide a
grounding of morality articulated through the idea of the categorical
imperative. What is remarkable here, from a standpoint such as
Nietzsche's, is that Kant should simply take our moral intuitions as
authoritative when the fact that we are characterized by these intuitions is the product of the particular contingent course of European
history. Indeed, it is precisely because Kant takes morality as a given
that he argues that we should not see human history as the product of
various contingent processes and struggles but, rather, *must* view it *as
if* it has a developmental logic, a providential structure (Kant 1991).
It is important to see that it is this way round for Kant. It is not his
developmental view of history that leads him to take our moral intuitions to be authoritative; it is his commitment to "morality" as a given
that leads Kant to the stance that it is practically *necessary* for us to be
committed to this view of history. This commitment to "morality" as
a given is also (and relatedly) illustrated by Kant's argument that we
must adopt "beliefs" in God, immortality of the soul and free will as
matters of faith (*res fidei*) since, he holds, these "beliefs" are necessary
conditions of maintaining a "moral" image of the world (Kant 1952:
§30 (91)). (Here Kant is promoting the role of these matters of faith
as what Wittgenstein would later call "hinge-propositions".)

We can be sure that Nietzsche noticed the implications of Kant's
argument: if these beliefs are discredited and can no longer play the
pivotal role that they have previously fulfilled, then the "moral" image
of the world collapses into *nihilism*: God is dead, everything is permitted. Here we find a second motivation for Nietzsche's pressing the
question of the value of morality, namely, the fear that the combination of seeing "morality" as the rational form of ethics and of scepticism towards the presuppositions of "morality" will lead to ethical
nihilism. It is, of course, the case that an alternative response to the
problems of Kant's moral philosophy would be to provide an account
that underwrites the authority of our moral intuitions and the conditions of maintaining a "moral" image of the world without recourse

to such matters of faith; this may be seen in Hegel's strategy in which Kant's judgement that we must view history *as if* it has a developmental logic is displaced by the argument that human history does actually have such a teleological structure. Once this move has been made, however, Nietzsche can point out that the reassurance that Hegel offers concerning the value and character of "morality" is dependent on the plausibility of his rational reconstruction of human history as exhibiting this teleological structure. In accordance with much of contemporary thought, Nietzsche does not find this reconstruction to be persuasive in comparison to the view that our history has the character of being composed of a motley assemblage of accidents, struggles, rationalizations and improvised responses to contingent events.

In contrast to his predecessors, then, Nietzsche does not attempt to offer a foundational account of morality but rather aims to treat it as a contingent historical artefact whose value can be coherently taken as an object of critical reflection. In adopting this stance, Nietzsche attempts to perform three tasks. First, he seeks to give a naturalistic account of morality. For Nietzsche, this requires that he account for the emergence of morality in non-moral terms and that his account should be compatible with our best *Wissenschaft* (i.e. our best systematic knowledge of the natural and cultural world as revealed by physics, chemistry, philology, archaeology, psychology, etc.). Nietzsche's naturalism is, importantly, non-reductive in that he does not rule out the employment of both general and culturally specific psychological features of human beings; he simply endeavours to draw on those features that do not depend on the presence of "morality". Put another way, we can say that Nietzsche aims to articulate a naturalism that seeks as far as possible to account for our current ethical psychology in terms ultimately drawn from other aspects of human psychology (see Williams 1995, 2000). Secondly, he endeavours to provide a historical account of the emergence and development of morality that makes perspicuous the diverse elements that have been yoked together to yield our current picture and practices of morality. Thirdly, he seeks to re-evaluate "morality" by providing *internal* reasons for us to question the value of our current moral values.

II

What then of the structure of the argument of this work? The book is divided into two parts. In Part I, I focus on reconstructing Nietzsche's route to a genealogical investigation of morality. In Part II, I turn to the structure and arguments of the *Genealogy* itself, addressing each essay in turn before reflecting on competing interpretations of the *Genealogy*. Let me sketch out the details of this framework a little more fully.

The introduction to Part I draws attention to the surprising fact that existing studies of the *Genealogy* have not addressed how Nietzsche comes to be committed to the project of re-evaluation or how developments in his understanding of the requirements of this project lead him to the kind of investigation that he carries out in the *Genealogy*. Yet it is clear that we shall be better placed to understand the philosophical purpose of the *Genealogy* and, indeed, of genealogy as a specific kind of philosophical enquiry, if we can reconstruct the philosophical context that leads to Nietzsche's development of this type of enquiry. Consequently, Chapter 1 provides an account of how Nietzsche moves from a project of the *devaluation* of morality to one of its *re-evaluation*. This account focuses in particular on Nietzsche's critical overcoming of Arthur Schopenhauer and Paul Rée as formative influences on his early work. Chapter 2 carries this developmental account further by focusing on three major problems that Nietzsche comes to identify with his initial understanding of, and attempt at, the project of re-evaluation. In this chapter, I try to show how meeting the challenges raised by these problems leads Nietzsche not only to acknowledge the need for the kind of critical enquiry that he will later characterize as "genealogy" but also to develop the philosophical resources required to engage in this type of enquiry. The final chapter of Part I retraces this process of development but from the standpoint of attention to Nietzsche's rhetorical strategies. In one respect, the purpose of this chapter is to support the arguments of the preceding chapters by showing that the shifts that have been detailed in the first two chapters map onto shifts in Nietzsche's rhetorical strategy in the ways that these arguments would suggest. However, this chapter is also designed to introduce the reader to the point that Nietzsche as a philosophical *writer* does not limit his reflective engagement with morality to the provision of good arguments but extends that engagement to consideration of how best to exhibit and mobilize the *force* of the reasons that he offers. This point matters because, in the *Genealogy* and elsewhere, Nietzsche does not want simply to set out a rational argument for our abstract and impartial consideration; he wants to *persuade* us – and, as we shall see, he takes that task to require that he engage our affects in a struggle that, whatever its final effects, will not leave us unchanged by the encounter with his work.

In the opening of Part II, I draw attention to the fact that Nietzsche does not understand himself to be the first practitioner of "genealogy", merely the first to engage in this practice with an appropriately historical spirit. This leads us in Chapter 4 to consider, in the light of Part I, how we should read the *Genealogy* and, in particular, I argue that we need to address this text in terms of a detailed specification of Nietzsche's target, the structure of his arguments and the operation of his rhetoric. Each of Chapters 5–7 then focuses on an essay of the *Genealogy*. Chapter 5 attends to Nietzsche's account of the slave revolt in morality with explicit attention to his focus on the transformation of both the understanding of moral agency and the good that is accomplished by this re-evaluation of noble morality. Chapter 6 analyses Nietzsche's accounts of the man of bad conscience, paying more regard than normal in treatments of this essay to the figure of the sovereign individual, and of the moralization of guilt. Chapter 7 elucidates Nietzsche's account and critique of the ascetic ideal, focusing on his explanation of the construction of "morality" in terms of unconditional commands of universal scope. In each of these chapters, I also draw attention to the ways in which Nietzsche sets up and then undermines certain expectations in his readers and the role that these rhetorical moves are intended to play with respect to his overall project. The final chapter of Part II addresses three competing views of Nietzsche's *Genealogy* offered by Brian Leiter, Raymond Geuss and Bernard Williams in order both to highlight the continuing debates over the character of this text and to defend my own view against significant challenges concerning the authority of Nietzsche's argument. I conclude by drawing attention to the relationship of Nietzsche's *Genealogy* to other more contemporary forms of historical philosophy.

PART ONE

The project of re-evaluation and the turn to genealogy

Introduction

It is a commonplace of contemporary Nietzsche scholarship to note
that Nietzsche's turn to genealogy is situated within the broader context of his project of a re-evaluation of values (see e.g. Ridley 1998a;
Geuss 1999a; May 1999; Leiter 2002). But what *specifically* motivates
Nietzsche's development of genealogy? Given the continuing debates
over the character of genealogy, debates that range over *what* genealogy is intended to do, for *whom* and *how* it is intended to achieve its
work,[1] one might suppose that Nietzsche's reasons for developing this
mode of enquiry would be subject to some scrutiny; after all, if we can
get clear about Nietzsche's reasons for turning to genealogy, we will
be well placed to understand what this mode of enquiry is intended
to accomplish. Yet what remains largely absent from contemporary
Nietzsche scholarship is any attention to the claims of a developmental approach that, in elucidating Nietzsche's reasons for turning to
genealogy, provides an interpretative basis for approaching *On the
Genealogy of Morality* itself. Part I of this study aims to supply this lack
by reconstructing the developmental context of the *Genealogy*.

We should note that a short response to this question concerning
his turn to genealogy is provided by Nietzsche himself in the preface to *On the Genealogy of Morality*, in which this development is
linked to his increasingly critical stance towards his "great teacher"
Schopenhauer[2] and his one-time friend Rée.[3] Here, Nietzsche tells us
that at the time of his initial encounter with Rée's work, while writing
Human, All Too Human (Part I), "my real concern was with something much more important than my own or anyone else's hypotheses about the origin of morality (or, to be more precise: the latter
interest was completely subordinate to a single goal to which it is

11

merely one among many means). For me, what was at stake was the *value* of morality" (GM Preface §5). This question was posed for him, Nietzsche reveals, in the context of his consideration of "the *value* of pity (*Mitleid*[4]) and of the morality of pity" endorsed by Schopenhauer (GM Preface §3). At issue here, Nietzsche recounts, "was the value of the 'unegoistic', the instincts of compassion, self-abnegation, self-sacrifice", which Schopenhauer presents as intrinsic, unconditional values and "on the basis of which he *said no* to life and also to himself" (GM Preface §5). Nietzsche continues:

> But it was against *these* very instincts that an increasingly fundamental suspicion, a skepticism which dug ever deeper, spoke out within me! It was here that I saw the *great* danger for mankind, its most sublime temptation and seduction – leading in what direction? towards nothingness? – It was here I saw the beginning of the end, the stagnation, the tired nostalgia, the will turning *against* life, the melancholy and tender signs of the approach of the last illness.   (*Ibid.*)

Nietzsche's suspicions are not entirely surprising when one considers Schopenhauer's philosophical stance. Schopenhauer's philosophical system starts from Kantian premises in that he begins by distinguishing between the realm of appearance (or representation) and the realm of the thing-in-itself; however, Schopenhauer notes that space and time as sensible intuitions that are constitutive of the possibility of individuating objects of experience belong to the realm of representation and, hence, the principle of individuation cannot legitimately be applied to the realm of the thing-in-itself. Schopenhauer then argues that we can have access to the realm of the world-in-itself through our awareness of ourselves as will and that will is the amorphous undifferentiated essence of the world-in-itself of which we, as individual wills, are the apparent (i.e. individuated) expressions. Yet will, on Schopenhauer's account, has no *telos* nor can it be satisfied; hence, as individuated expressions of will, we are characterized by continuous cravings that can never be sated. Happiness is merely a necessarily temporary cessation of suffering. Schopenhauer's pessimism finds its most forceful expression in his endorsement of the wisdom of Silenus: the best is not to have been born, the next best is to die young. The subjection to suffering that necessarily follows our conditions as individuals characterized by willing can only be overcome in those forms of experience in which we are detached from willing. Aesthetic experience, on Schopenhauer's account, is the exemplary form of the experience of ourselves as "will-free". In relation to morality, this system unsurprisingly finds expression in the identification of morality with compassion (*Mitleid*), that is, with the altruistic selflessness to which Nietzsche draws attention. Thus, while accepting Kant's argument for the claim that self-interested action cannot have moral value, Schopenhauer proposes, in stark contrast to Kant (in relation to whom he anticipates Nietzsche's recognition of the dependency of Kant's ethics of duty on discredited theological commitments; see Cartwright 1998: 123), that the fundamental basis of morality is pity or compassion. For Nietzsche, who accepts much of Schopenhauer's critique of Kant, the problem posed by Schopenhauer's thought is not simply that Schopenhauer also accepts morality as a given, but that this morality of compassion is an expression of Schopenhauer's hostility to our creaturely existence.

This might seem to be a problem that is restricted to the kind of moral philosophy endorsed by Schopenhauer; however, while, as Nietzsche acknowledges, the problem of the value of compassion and of the morality of compassion "seems at first glance an isolated issue, a free-standing question-mark", Nietzsche suggests that this impression is not sustained:

> But whoever pauses here, whoever *learns* to ask questions here, will undergo the same experience as I – that of a huge new prospect opening up, a vertiginous possibility, as every kind of mistrust, suspicion, and fear leaps forward, and the belief in morality, all morality, falters. Finally, a new demand finds expression. Let us articulate this *new demand*: we stand in need of a *critique* of moral values, *the value of these values itself should first of all be called into question.*
>
> (GM Preface §6)

Nietzsche's intuition, in other words, is that Schopenhauer's morality of compassion is an expression of our moral values and in so far as we find reasons to be concerned about the value of the morality of compassion, we are led to raise the question of the value of morality, of our moral values, more generally.

What addressing this demand requires with respect to values is "a knowledge of the conditions and circumstances of their growth, development, displacement", a "knowledge the like of which has never before existed nor even been desired" (*ibid.*). More particularly, it requires "a more correct method of arriving at the answers" in which "a sharp and impartial eye" is pointed in "the direction of the real *history of morality*" instead of towards "English hypothesizing *into the blue*" (GM Preface §7). Genealogy, as he practises it, is conceived by Nietzsche as the "more correct method" needed to provide this new kind of knowledge. It is important to note that in stressing the need for a historical account of morality and contrasting this with "English hypothesizing *into the blue*", Nietzsche is signalling his opposition to the kind of reflections on the origin of morality provided by his erstwhile friend Paul Rée, who had sought to give just such an account in *The Origin of the Moral Sensations*. Influenced by Hume and Darwin, as well as Nietzsche himself,[5] Rée had tried to offer an evolutionary account of ethics in terms of group selection and there is little doubt that Nietzsche was, at the time of writing *Human, All Too Human*, much taken with Rée's work. Thus, as Robin Small (2003: xxxv) has pointed out, in the second volume of *Human, All Too Human*, entitled "The Wanderer and his Shadow", Nietzsche offers an unacknowledged paraphrase of Rée's central argument as an argument of his own:

> The same actions that within primitive society were first performed with a view to common *utility* have later been performed by other generations from other motives: out of fear or reverence of those who demanded and recommended them, or out of habit, because one had seen them done all around one from childhood on, or out of benevolence, because their performance generally produced joy and approving faces, or out of vanity, because they were commended. Such actions, whose basic motive, that of utility, has been *forgotten* are then called *moral* actions: not because, for instance, they are performed out of those *other* motives, but because they are *not* performed from any conscious reason of utility. (WS §40)

Somewhat brazenly, it is precisely this form of reasoning that Nietzsche will attack in the first essay of the *Genealogy* as an example of how "English" philosophizing about morality goes wrong. Notably, in a rather backhanded compliment to Rée, the first two essays of the *Genealogy* – "'Good and Evil', 'Good and Bad'" and "'Guilt', 'Bad Conscience' and Related Matters" – echo and adapt the titles of the opening essays of Rée's *The Origin of Moral Sensations*, namely, "The Origin of the Concepts 'Good' and 'Evil'" and "The Origin of Conscience".

On this autobiographical account, then, Nietzsche's turn to genealogy is motivated by his commitment to the ethical project of a re-evaluation of our values conducted through a naturalistic account of the historical conditions of the emergence and development of morality. This fragment of intellectual autobiography thus provides some signposts for our enquiry, but it is hardly sufficient for our purposes. Reconstructing the reasons for Nietzsche's turn to, and development of, genealogy requires that we show how, and why, Nietzsche comes to see re-evaluation as a necessary project that requires the provision of naturalistic historical accounts of morality. To address these issues is the task of the following three chapters. Chapter 1 offers a developmental account of how Nietzsche comes to conceive of the project of a re-evaluation and Chapter 2 focuses on the development of his understanding of the nature and demands of this project. Chapter 3 tracks the shifts in his rhetorical strategy that accompany his developing conception of the task of re-evaluation; it offers both indirect support for the account given in the preceding chapters and an illustration of the centrality of a philosophically motivated concern with giving adequate rhetorical expression to his arguments in Nietzsche's project.

CHAPTER ONE

Towards the project of re-evaluation

The route by which Nietzsche comes to conceive of a project of re-evaluation can be reconstructed in terms of his increasing rejection of specific features of the influence exercised by Schopenhauer and, to a lesser extent, Paul Rée over his thinking. The influence of the former is hard to exaggerate, as Nietzsche himself acknowledges (see UM III; Janaway 1998c), but it is equally hard to overlook Nietzsche's subjection of his inheritance from Schopenhauer to a process of critical reflection characterized by the increasingly deep disavowal of the terms of that inheritance. It is, at any rate, within the terms of this critical relationship to Schopenhauer that Nietzsche comes to conceive of the possibility of the project of a re-evaluation of values, and I shall begin by tracing Nietzsche's overcoming of these features, before laying out the initial form of his project of re-evaluation.

I

Nietzsche's 1868 essay "On Schopenhauer" indicates that he is already well aware of the problems with, and objections to, Schopenhauer's metaphysics of the will and is thus by no means an uncritical disciple of this philosopher.[1] Even in *The Birth of Tragedy*, which is typically taken to be Nietzsche's most explicitly Schopenhauerian text, Nietzsche's appropriation of Schopenhauer's philosophy is already characterized by a certain critical distance. Thus, while the central distinction between the Dionysian and Apollonian of that work expresses, in eccentric fashion, Schopenhauer's distinction between the world as will and as representation, Nietzsche's use of Schopenhauer is mediated through Friedrich Lange's neo-Kantian concept of the "standpoint of the ideal", which allowed him to treat Schopenhauer's ideas as fictitious but unifying metaphysical concepts (Salaquarda 1998: 101). At the same time, Nietzsche's ethical stance in *The Birth of Tragedy* already exhibits the distrust of Schopenhauer's morality of pity referred to in the preface to the *Genealogy*. Thus, while Nietzsche endorses the descriptive aspect of Schopenhauer's pessimism, he rejects the evaluative and recommendatory aspects of this pessimism, drawing a distinction between a pessimism of weakness (Schopenhauer) and a pessimism of strength (the Greek tragedians).[2] The first step away from Schopenhauer expressed in these two critical reflections on his "great teacher" finds further expression in his 1874 essay "Schopenhauer as Educator", in which Nietzsche already presents Schopenhauer as an exemplary human being rather than a philosophical authority. Looking back on this essay in 1886, Nietzsche remarks:

> When, in the third *Untimely Meditation*, I then went on to give expression to my reverence for my first and only educator, the *great* Arthur Schopenhauer ... I was, so far as my own development was concerned, already deep in the midst of the moral skepticism and destructive analysis, *that is to say in the critique and likewise the intensifying of pessimism as understood hitherto*, and already "believed in nothing any more", as the people put it, not even in Schopenhauer.
>
> (WS Preface §1)

This "moral skepticism and destructive analysis" comes to expression in *Human, All Too Human*, in which Nietzsche comes to take the second of his steps away from Schopenhauer through a critique of metaphysical philosophy articulated in terms of a turn to a naturalistic mode of historical philosophy in which scientific knowledge is privileged, a turn that was significantly influenced by his friendship with Rée (HAH §§1–3, see also Small 2003). Nietzsche's theoretical aim in this work is to distance his position from, and demonstrate the superfluousness of, the idea of a metaphysical world expressed in Schopenhauer's philosophy. He adopts two main tactics for achieving this strategic goal.

Nietzsche's first tactic is to present general arguments to the effect that (i) although "the absolute possibility" of a metaphysical world "is hardly to be disputed", we can have no knowledge of it and, even if we could have knowledge of it, such knowledge would be useless (HAH

§9), and (ii) the thought that we can have knowledge of the metaphysical world and that such knowledge is the most valuable kind of knowledge is the product of "passion, error and self-deception" (*ibid.*). Thus, for example, Nietzsche argues that the idea of a metaphysical realm initially emerges on the basis of experiences such as dreams (HAH §5). This idea is then deployed to support, for example, our belief in free will, a belief that is itself "a primary error" (HAH §18): part of a picture of the world that is "the outcome of a host of errors and fantasies which have gradually arisen and grown entwined with one another in the course of the overall evolution of the organic being, and are now inherited by us as the accumulated treasure of the entire past – as treasure: for the value of our humanity depends on it" (HAH §16). It is only "very late" in the evolution of our cognitive abilities that science emerges as a counter to such metaphysical thinking that is, to a limited extent, "capable of detaching us from this ideational world" (*ibid.*). Such arguments aim at establishing that metaphysics is "the science that treats of the fundamental errors of mankind – but does so as though they were fundamental truths" (HAH §18).

Nietzsche's second tactic is to show that religion, art and morality, whose higher value is explained by recourse to a metaphysical realm (HAH §1), have no justifiable claim to put us "in touch with the world's heart", that is, the metaphysical world (HAH §4). Their value can be accounted for in straightforwardly naturalistic terms and this – once realized – ensures that "the greater part of our interest in the purely theoretical problem of the 'thing in itself' and 'appearance' ceases to exist" (HAH §10). In Humean fashion, Nietzsche argues that our beliefs and sentiments arise not from reason but from sensations of pleasure and pain (HAH §18) and that the supposedly "higher" motives expressed in religion, art and morality are sublimated expressions of human, all too human motivations. In particular, following La Rochefoucauld (HAH §35)[3] and Rée (HAH §§36–7), Nietzsche argues against Schopenhauer that so-called "unegoistic" motives for action are, at root, expressions of psychological egoism. In effect, then, Nietzsche accepts Schopenhauer's evaluative ranking of unegoistic (higher) and egoistic (lower) motivations but denies the existence of the former. As Maudemarie Clark and Leiter put it: "*Human, All Too Human*'s psychological egoism amounts to a claim that we can explain human behavior without appeal to a reality lying beyond the natural or phenomenal world, combined with Schopenhauer's assumption that all motivation in the latter world is egoistic" (1997: xxiv). Taken together, these tactics aim to show that metaphysics "is inspired by error in so far as it aims to explain the existence of things (1) that we erroneously believe to exist and (2) that we erroneously believe cannot be explained by empirical methods" (Clark 1998: 50).

Yet, as the remark by Clark and Leiter indicates, the terms in which Nietzsche conducts his turn to historical philosophy are still significantly drawn from Schopenhauer and can be understood in terms of a Schopenhauerian philosophy stripped of its metaphysical commitments (see *ibid*.).[4] The crucial feature of this step for our concerns is that Nietzsche's Rée-influenced turn to naturalism is linked at this stage to a commitment to psychological egoism and, concomitantly, a denial of moral motivations that he still understands in Schopenhauerian terms as essentially "unegoistic" in character. Nietzsche's remark in the preface to the *Genealogy* that he was concerned at the point at which he encountered Rée's work with the value of the morality of compassion needs to be understood in this context. The Nietzsche of *Human, All Too Human* accepts (i) Schopenhauer's critique of Kant to the effect that the moral worth of an action is rooted in its expression of compassion rather than duty and (ii) Schopenhauer's conclusion that actions motivated by egoism can have no moral worth, but follows Rée in arguing (iii) that all actions are motivated by egoism in more or less sublimated form.[5] At this stage, then, Nietzsche cannot conceive of the project of a *re-evaluation* of moral values but only of the project of a *devaluation* of morality (see Ridley 2005 on this point).

The final step necessary for Nietzsche to conceive of the project of re-evaluation comes in *Daybreak*, which, as Nietzsche tells us in *Ecce Homo*, marks the point at which his "campaign against morality" through the project of "a *revaluation of all values*" begins (EH "Why I Write Such Good Books", on *Daybreak*). The crucial move is Nietzsche's rejection of Schopenhauer's identification of moral actions with actions that are necessarily characterized by altruistic motives. Thus, Nietzsche argues that if we identify moral actions with actions "performed for the sake of another and only for his sake" (or, alternatively, and here Nietzsche extends his remarks to include Kant, with actions "which are performed out of freedom of will") then there are "no moral actions!" But, he contends, the definition of morality in these terms is "the effect of certain intellectual mistakes" that have led us to overestimate the value of certain kinds of action at the expense of others. By realigning these "moral" actions with "the 'egoistic' and 'unfree' actions", Nietzsche argues, "we shall restore to men their goodwill towards the actions decried as egoistic and restore to these actions their *value – we shall deprive them of their bad conscience!*"

(D §148). To establish this argument, Nietzsche proposes an account of the origin of morality that has the following features:

- It identifies moral action with conduct according to custom (D §9).
- It argues that customs are expressions of a community's relationship with its environment that evaluate and rank types of action in terms of their utility or harmfulness with respect to the self-preservation of the community (*ibid.*; see also GS §116).
- It suggests that early societies are characterized by superfluous customs that play the role of inculcating the rule of obeying rules (D §16).
- It claims that the morality of customs is predicated on belief in imaginary causalities (D §10; see also §§21, 24).
- It argues that the system of moral judgements that expresses the evaluation and ranking of types of action structures our human drives in composing a second nature characterized by a system of moral sentiments that governs our moral agency (D §38; see also §99).

This account of the origin of morality provides a way for Nietzsche to reject Schopenhauer's identification of moral action and unegoistic action as well as Kant's metaphysics of morals through an argument that looks remarkably like a naturalization of Kant's account of reverence for moral law. As Clark and Leiter note:

> Despite a slight difference in terminology, Nietzsche's description of the most primitive form of moral motivation closely follows Kant's description of reverence. Kant's "reverence for the law" in effect becomes "obedience to tradition," while Kant's "immediate determination by" and "subordination of my will to a law without mediation" becomes obedience to "a higher authority ... not because it commands what would be *useful* for one to do, but simply because it commands".
> (Clark & Leiter 1997: xxx–xxi, quoting D §9)[6]

While Nietzsche's sketch of the origin of morality does not account for how we have come to be characterized by the "intellectual mistakes" that lead us to identify morality with actions performed out of freedom of will or purely altruistic motives, it supplies a basis on which such an account could be constructed once it is supplemented by the hypotheses on moral innovation,[7] on the construction of belief in a metaphysical world (see e.g. D §33) and on the historical causes of the spread of the morality of pity (D §132) that Nietzsche adduces. The crucial point for our current concerns is that Nietzsche argues that Christian morality is continuous with the morality of custom in respect of being predicated on belief in imaginary causalities; a point Nietzsche illustrates by reference to the Christian belief that suffering – and existence in so far as it inevitably involves suffering – is to be construed as punishment for our sinful or guilty natures (see D §§13, 76–80, 86).

The conclusion that Nietzsche draws from this set of arguments is presented thus:

> *There are two kinds of deniers of morality.* – "To deny moral-
> ity" – this can mean, *first*, to deny that the moral motives
> which men claim have inspired their actions have really done
> so – it is thus the assertion that morality consists of words and
> is among the coarser or more subtle deceptions (especially
> self-deceptions) which men practise, and perhaps so espe-
> cially in precisely the case of those most famed for virtue.
> *Then* it can mean: to deny that moral judgments are based
> on truths. Here it is admitted that they really are motives for
> action, but that in this way it is *errors* which, as the basis of all
> moral judgment, impel men to their moral actions. This is *my*
> point of view: though I should be the last to deny that *in very
> many cases* there is some ground for suspicion that the other
> point of view – that is to say, the point of La Rochefocauld
> and others who think like him – may also be justified and in
> any event of great general application. – Thus I deny moral-
> ity as I deny alchemy, that is, I deny their premises: but I do
> *not* deny that there have been alchemists who believed in
> these premises and acted in accordance with them. – I also
> deny immorality: *not* that countless people *feel* themselves
> to be immoral but that there is any *true* reason so to feel. It
> goes without saying that I do not deny – unless I am a fool
> – that many actions called immoral ought to be avoided and
> resisted, or that many called moral ought to be done and
> encouraged – but I think that one should be encouraged and
> the other avoided *for other reasons than hitherto*. We have to
> *learn to think differently* – in order at last, perhaps very late
> on, to attain even more: *to feel differently*.   (D §103)[8]

Thus, Nietzsche conceives of the project of a re-evaluation of values as a project in which moral values can be re-evaluated as *moral* (i.e. *intrinsic*) *values* and not merely as expressions of self-interest:

> Nietzsche presents the project of re-evaluation as a critique of the structure of reasons immanent in a given way of living, a structure that the values intrinsic to that way of living hold in place. And that, evidently enough, is a very different project from La Rochfoucauld's. (Ridley 2005: 176)

II

On the initial understanding of this project developed in *Daybreak*, Nietzsche takes its requirements to be threefold:

- to demonstrate that Christianity is predicated on belief in imaginary causalities in order to undermine the epistemic authority of Christian morality (D §§13, 76–80, 86);
- to mobilize the affects cultivated by Christian morality against that morality in order to undermine its affective power (see e.g. D §§78, 131, 199);
- to recommend an alternative (largely Greek) morality (see e.g. D §§199, 556).[9]

It is notable that these requirements are closely related in Nietzsche's practice in that a large part of the immanent strategy of critique in *Daybreak* involves exploiting the view expressed in Schopenhauer's morality of pity to the effect that suffering is intrinsically bad in order to argue that Greek morality is superior to Christian morality from this point of view.

Thus, for example, Nietzsche advances the claim that Christian morality is objectionable in terms of its reliance on false causalities on the grounds that it is characterized by an interpretation of suffering – and, indeed, of existence (since suffering is an inevitable feature of it) – as punishment (D §13). Highlighting the erroneous but pivotal Christian idea that misfortune is the punishment (effect) of sin (cause), Nietzsche argues that such a schema of interpretation has "robbed of its innocence the whole purely chance character of events … it is as though the education of the human race had hitherto been directed by the fantasies of jailers and hangmen" (D §13; see also D

§§77–9). What is ethically objectionable about this Christian-moral interpretation of suffering is that it intensifies the suffering to which the agent is subject by treating the occasion of extensional suffering (suffering that is independent of the fact of human self-consciousness, e.g. breaking a leg) as itself a source of intensional suffering (suffering that is dependent on the fact of human self-consciousness, e.g. God's punishment of one's sins) that is of potentially much greater magnitude than the extensional suffering on which it supervenes.[10] In contrast, Greek morality allows for "pure innocent misfortune", in which the occasion of extensional suffering of the agent is precisely *not* a source of intensional suffering (see D §78 for a clear statement of this point). In this respect, if one holds – as, for example, Schopenhauer does – that suffering is intrinsically bad, then the fact that Greek morality reduces the overall amount of suffering in the world is an argument for Greek ethics.

Notice, though, that in pursuing this strategy of immanent critique, Nietzsche takes himself to be limited to recommending an alternative (Greek) ideal to that of Christianity. His reason is that while he thinks we can all agree that "the goal of morality is defined in approximately the following way: it is the preservation and advancement of mankind" (D §106), he can see no way of specifying the substantive content of this goal that is not tendentious (see D §§106, 139). We shall return to this point in the next chapter.

Conclusion

In this chapter we have seen how Nietzsche arrived at the project of re-evaluation through a gradual process of surmounting the influence of Schopenhauer and Rée on his thinking, and we have briefly sketched the form that this project took in *Daybreak*. Three features of this initial formulation of the project are particularly worth stressing. The first is that Nietzsche is utterly explicit that this project does not require the rejection of all the kinds of conduct that we call "moral" or the encouragement of all the kinds of conduct that we call "immoral":

> It goes without saying that I do not deny – unless I am a fool – that many actions called immoral ought to be avoided and resisted, or that many called moral ought to be done and encouraged – but I think that one should be encouraged and the other avoided *for other reasons than hitherto*. (D §103)

The second is that Nietzsche does not simply juxtapose his preferred morality to that of Christianity; instead he offers a form of immanent critique of the latter that works to the comparative advantage of the former. In other words, even at this early stage in his development of the project of re-evaluation, Nietzsche acknowledges that the plausibility of his project requires that he provide *internal* reasons to his audience to reject "morality".

The final feature to note is that Nietzsche regards his articulation of the project of re-evaluation in *Daybreak* as a preliminary development:

> *Moral interregnum.* – Who would now be in a position to describe that which will one day *do away with* moral feelings and judgments! – however sure one may be that the foundations of the latter are all defective and their superstructure is beyond repair: their obligatory force must diminish from day to day, so long as the obligatory force of reason does not diminish! To construct anew the laws of life and action – for this task our sciences of physiology, medicine, sociology and solitude are not yet sufficiently sure of themselves: and it is from them that the foundation-stones of new ideals (if not the new ideals themselves) must come. So it is that, according to our taste and talent, we live an existence which is either a *prelude* or a *postlude*, and the best we can do in this *interregnum* is to be as far as possible our own *reges* and found little *experimental states*. We are experiments: let us also want to be them! (D §453)

In the *Genealogy*, Nietzsche will offer what he also describes as preliminary studies towards a re-evaluation of our moral values. However, to see how we get to that event requires that we turn to look at how Nietzsche developed and refined the project of re-evaluation.

CHAPTER TWO

Revising the project of re-evaluation

While *Daybreak* marks the initiation of the project of re-evaluation, Nietzsche's work in *The Gay Science* and in *Beyond Good and Evil* represents a process of development and revision in his understanding of the nature of this task. Specifically, Nietzsche gradually identifies three major problems:

- His analysis in *Daybreak* had presupposed that the loss of belief in God would lead directly to a loss of authority of Christian moral beliefs; although people would still act *as if* this morality were authoritative in that they would still, at least for a time, be characterized by the moral sentiments cultivated by Christianity, they would no longer accept the authority of the moral beliefs characteristic of Christianity. However, Nietzsche comes to see this assumption as problematic. By the time of composing Book III of *The Gay Science* it appears to him that his contemporaries, while increasingly characterized by atheism, do not understand this loss of faith to undermine the authority of Christian morality. It is not that they act in accordance with morality while no longer believing in it, but that they still believe in morality, that is, they take the authority of Christian morality to be unaffected by the fact that they no longer believe in God.
- In *Daybreak*, Nietzsche had taken the authority of scientific knowledge for granted in making his case. However, he comes to acknowledge that this cannot simply be assumed given the constraint of naturalism that characterizes his project and given that he requires a naturalistic account of how we come to value truth and why this should lead us to reject Christian morality.

- With the exception of his remarks on suffering, the account in *Daybreak* had failed to provide any compelling basis for re-evaluating moral values that did not simply express Nietzsche's own evaluative commitments. Nietzsche comes to see this problem as related to the inadequacy of his account of how we come to be committed to Christian morality at all since, as he will later stress in *Beyond Good and Evil*, the establishment of Christianity promised "a revaluation of all the values of antiquity" (BGE §46).

Addressing these problems leads Nietzsche to revise significantly his view of the nature and requirements of the project of re-evaluation.

I

Nietzsche's perception of the first of these problems is manifest in Book III of *The Gay Science*, which famously opens with the announcement "God is dead; but given the way people are, there may still for millennia be caves in which they show his shadow. – And we – we must still defeat his shadow as well!" (GS §108).[1] The problem that Nietzsche identifies – what might be called the problem of *not inferring* (i.e. of failing to draw appropriate conclusions in virtue of being held captive by a picture or perspective) – and dramatizes in "*Der tolle Mensch*" (§125), is that while his contemporaries are increasingly coming to surrender belief in God, they do not draw the implication from this that Nietzsche insists follows. As he will later put this point in *Twilight of the Idols*:

> When one gives up Christian belief one thereby deprives oneself of the *right* to Christian morality. For the latter is absolutely *not* self-evident: one must make this point again and again, in spite of English shallowpates. Christianity is a system, a consistently thought out and *complete* view of things. If one breaks out of it a fundamental idea, the belief in God, one thereby breaks the whole thing to pieces: one has nothing of any consequence left in one's hands. ... – it [the system] stands or falls with the belief in God.
>
> (TI "Expeditions of an Untimely Man" §5)[2]

Nietzsche describes this phenomenon of *not inferring* as follows:

But in the main one may say: The event [that "God is dead"] is far too great, too distant, too remote from the multitude's capacity for comprehension even for the tidings of it to be thought of as having *arrived* as yet. Much less may one suppose that many people know as yet *what* this event really means – and how much must collapse now that this faith has been undermined because it was built upon this faith, propped up by it, grown into it: for example, the whole of our European morality. (GS §343)

There are two aspects to this: first, the character of our morality has been shaped by our Christian faith and its authority underwritten by that faith; secondly, this is not understood by Nietzsche's contemporaries. As James Conant puts it:

> those who do not believe in God are able to imagine that the death of God marks nothing more than a change in what people should now "believe". One should now subtract the belief in God from one's body of beliefs; and this subtraction is something sophisticated people (who have long since ceased going to church) can effect without unduly upsetting how they live or what they value. (1995: 262)

Nietzsche thus recognizes the need for two related tasks: first, to provide an account of this phenomenon of *not inferring* and, secondly, to find a way of demonstrating that the inference that he draws is the appropriate one.

In approaching the first of these tasks, Nietzsche has in his sights once again the example of Schopenhauer, who exhibits precisely the stance of combining "admitted and uncompromising atheism" with "staying stuck in those Christian and ascetic moral perspectives" (GS §357).[3] Nietzsche's use of this example suggests that the problem of *not inferring* arises from the fact that his contemporaries remain committed to a metaphysical stance towards the world that is "not the origin of religion, as Schopenhauer has it, but only a *late offshoot* of it" (GS §151). This metaphysical stance is to be understood as a product of philosophy conducted "under the seduction of morality" (D Preface §3; see also BGE §§2 and 5) in that it is commitment to the unconditional authority of (Christian) morality that finds expression in the construction of a metaphysical perspective, that is, a perspective that denies its own perspectival character.[4] We do not draw the appropriate implications from the death of God because we are held captive by a metaphysical perspective according to which the source and authority of our values is entirely independent of us.[5] It is, I take it, part of Nietzsche's point when, in "The Scope of the Moral" in *The Gay Science*, he remarks that there "are no experiences other than moral ones, not even in the realm of sense-perception" (GS §114), to suggest that our epistemic perspective on the world is governed by our moral perspective on the world and, hence, that the claim of our moral perspective to unconditional validity will find articulation in conceptions of ontology, epistemology and philosophical anthropology that support and express this claim.[6] In this context, Nietzsche's second task, that of showing that the death of God does have the implications that he claims, requires that he provide a naturalistic account of our morality that demonstrates how we have become subject to this taste for the unconditional – "the worst possible taste" (BGE §31), as Nietzsche calls it – and, hence, subject to the allure of this metaphysical perspective. It also requires that he show how it has become possible for us to free ourselves from this picture (and, indeed, this taste) and why we are compelled to do so.

These latter points are closely connected to Nietzsche's engagement with the second problem that he comes to discern with his understanding of his project in *Daybreak*, namely, the need to give a naturalistic account of our commitment to the unconditional value of truth.

II

Nietzsche's engagement with the topic of truth is complex but, for our purposes, the salient points are, first, that Nietzsche, at least in his mature work, is committed to the view that one can have beliefs, make statements and so on that are true or false (see Clark 1990; Gemes 1992; Leiter 1994) and, secondly, that we are characterized by a commitment to the unconditional value of truth. In respect of Nietzsche's perspectivism, we may merely note that this doctrine – itself a product of Nietzsche's naturalizing of epistemology – is compatible with commitment to the concept of truth: a perspective determines what is intelligibly up for grabs as true-or-false, *not* what is true-or-false. Our concern, though, is with the issue raised by Nietzsche in response to the shortcomings of *Daybreak*, namely, how we come to be characterized by a commitment to the unconditional value of truth. A tentative approach to this issue is given expression in Book III of *The Gay Science*, in which Nietzsche suggests that the concept of knowledge arose originally as a way of endorsing certain basic beliefs that are useful (i.e. species-preserving) errors but that eventually "knowledge and the striving for the true finally took their place as needs among the other needs" and:

> knowledge became a part of life, a continually growing power, until finally knowledge and the ancient basic errors struck against each other, both as life, both as power, both in the same person ... after the drive to truth has *proven* itself to be life-preserving power, too. (GS §110)

The problem with this argument is that it cannot account for the unconditional character of our will to truth, our conviction "that truth is more important than anything else, than every other conviction" (GS §344). Thus, Nietzsche argues, in the fifth book of *The Gay Science* added five years later:

> Precisely this conviction could never have originated if truth *and* untruth had constantly made it clear that they were both useful, as they are. So, the faith in science, which after all undeniably exists, cannot owe its origin to such a calculus of utility; rather it must have originated *in spite of* the fact that the disutility and dangerousness of "the will to truth" or "truth at any price" is proved to it constantly. Consequently, "will to truth" does *not* mean "I do not want to let myself be deceived" but – there is no alternative – "I will not deceive, not even myself"; *and with that we stand on moral ground.*
> (*Ibid.*)

So if Nietzsche is to give a satisfying account of how we come to be characterized by our faith in the unconditional value of truth, this will have to be integrated into his account of the formation of Christian morality. Notice though that while it is our faith in science that is to compel us to abandon our religious and, more importantly, moral commitments and, hence, to recognize the necessity of a re-evaluation of values, appeal to our faith in science cannot do all the work necessary since this faith in science is itself an expression of the morality whose value Nietzsche is concerned to call into question. As Nietzsche acknowledges:

> But you will have gathered what I am getting at, namely, that
> it is still a *metaphysical faith* upon which our faith in sci-
> ence rests – that even we knowers of today, we godless anti-
> metaphysicians, still take *our* fire, too, from the thousand-year
> old faith, the Christian faith which was also Plato's faith, that
> God is truth; that truth is divine ... (*Ibid.*)[7]

With these remarks Nietzsche both situates his own philosophical
activity within the terms of the death of God and acknowledges that if
he is to demonstrate the necessity of a re-evaluation of our moral values,
this must include a demonstration of the need for a re-evaluation of the
value of truth that appeals to nothing more than our existing motivational set in its stripped down form, that is, our will to truth. If Nietzsche
can provide such an account, he will have resolved one dimension of
the problem of authority that confronts his project since he will have
demonstrated that the necessity of the re-evaluation of Christian morality with respect to its claim concerning the unconditioned character
of its highest values is derived from the central commitments of that
morality itself. However, as Nietzsche acknowledges (see GS §346),
accomplishing this task does itself raise a further potential threat, the
threat of nihilism, which we can gloss in Dostoevsky's terms: God is
dead, everything is permitted. To avoid this threat, Nietzsche needs to
provide an account of how we can stand to ourselves as moral agents, as
agents committed to, and bound by, moral values, that does not require
recourse to a metaphysical perspective. This issue is closely related to
the third of the problems that Nietzsche identifies with *Daybreak*.

III

In Nietzsche's responses to both of the preceding problems that he
identifies with his understanding of his project of re-evaluation in
Daybreak, he has had to recognize that the requirements of this project
involve providing a compelling account of how we have become subject to Christian morality as a morality that both involves a particular
ranking of values and claims an unconditional authority. In approaching the third problem that he identifies with *Daybreak*, namely, the
need for well-grounded naturalistic criteria for evaluating moral
values, Nietzsche confronts the other dimension of the problem of
authority that bedevils his project. We can put it this way: even if
Nietzsche finds a way of demonstrating that we should disavow the

unconditional status claimed by Christian morality and, hence, demonstrates that we cannot value Christian morality for the (metaphysical) reasons that we have hitherto endorsed, this would not suffice to provide a criterion in terms of which our valuing should be conducted. Moreover, Nietzsche comes to see that this problem is connected to another problem, namely, his inability to give an adequate account in *Daybreak* of the motivation for, and success of, the re-evaluation of the values of antiquity accomplished by Christianity.

What connects this explanatory problem to Nietzsche's evaluative problem is that, *at a general and abstract level*, Nietzsche's concern to translate man back into nature (see GS §110 and BGE §230) entails that his account of the motivation for a re-evaluation of Christian morality must be continuous with his account of the motivation for the Christian re-evaluation of the morality of antiquity. Both the re-evaluation accomplished by Christianity and the re-evaluation proposed by Nietzsche need, in other words, to be explicable in terms of basic features of human beings as natural creatures in order to exhibit the right kind of continuity. To the extent that Nietzsche has an official candidate for this role in *Daybreak* and the original edition of *The Gay Science*, it is self-preservation (see GS §116 and D §19). However, there is a problem with this candidate in that it does not obviously fit well with forms of human activity that risk or, indeed, aim at self-destruction on the part of individuals and communities. To put the same point another way, it does not seem well poised to account for forms of growth or expansion on the part of individuals or communities that are not directed to developing resources for self-preservation or, indeed, make self-preservation more difficult.[8] While Nietzsche acknowledges that self-preservation can be a powerful motive for action, this limitation leads him to propose another candidate: *will to power*.[9]

The doctrine of will to power is proposed by Nietzsche as a general hypothesis concerning life:

> Physiologists should think twice before positioning the drive for self-preservation as the cardinal drive of an organic being. Above all, a living thing wants to *discharge* its strength – life itself is will to power –: self-preservation is only one of the indirect and most frequent *consequences* of this.
> (BGE §13; cf. GS §349)[10]

The basic claim involved in this hypothesis is that organic creatures are governed by an architectonic interest in the feeling of power, a feeling that they experience (to various degrees) in overcoming obstacles to growth. Hence *flourishing* for living creatures consists in the continuous heightening of the feeling of power, that is, in the continual overcoming of (increasingly resistant) obstacles to growth. Life is the expression of power in this sense.[11] Whatever the merits of this hypothesis as a hypothesis concerning organic life in general, it provides the theoretical context for Nietzsche's translation of human beings back into nature.

Nietzsche argues that human beings are continuous with other organic creatures in terms of being characterized by will to power, that is, in being governed by an architectonic interest in the feeling of power. It should be noted that this does not imply that human beings aim directly at the feeling of power but, rather, that the activity of overcoming various obstacles to the achievement of specific ends produces the feeling of power and, since through such activity human beings enjoy the self-reflexive experience of power, this leads to the valuing of forms of activity that support and enhance, and the devaluing of forms of activity that undermine and diminish, the feeling of power.[12] However, and this point is fundamental to Nietzsche's argument, he also stresses that the fact that human beings are characterized by self-consciousness entails that they are distinct from other organic creatures in two crucial respects.

First, the character of the *feeling* of power (or powerlessness) can take an astonishingly wide range of forms (e.g. cheerfulness, pity, benevolence, contempt) and vary across a number of axes (e.g. intensity, duration and depth). Secondly, *(the degree of) the feeling of power* that human beings experience need have no necessary connection to the *(degree of) power* expressed. Nietzsche's point is this: because human beings are self-conscious creatures, the feeling of power to which their doings give rise is necessarily mediated by the perspective in terms of which they understand (or misunderstand) themselves as agents and the moral evaluation and ranking of types of action expressed within that perspective. Consequently, an expansion (or diminution) of the feeling of power can be an effect of a change of perspective rather than of an actual increase (or decrease) of power expressed.[13] A clear illustration of this point is provided in *The Gay Science*:

> The true invention of the religion-founders is first to establish a certain way of life and everyday customs that work as a *disciplina voluntatis* while at the same time removing

boredom; and then to give just this life an *interpretation* that makes it appear illuminated by the highest worth, so that henceforth it becomes a good for which one fights and under certain circumstances even gives one's life. Actually, the second invention is the more important: the first, the way of life, was usually in place, though alongside other ways of life and without any consciousness of its special worth. (GS §353)[14]

Under such conditions of perspective change, Nietzsche makes plain, the feeling of power attendant on the exercise of one's capacities within a given way of life can be wholly transformed without any change in one's doings, that is, one's actual capacities and their exercise. (An important instance of such perspective change is the slave revolt in morality that is discussed by Nietzsche in the first essay of the *Genealogy*, which I shall address in Chapter 5). Furthermore, as Paul Patton points out: "If Nietzsche's conception of human being as governed by the drive to enhance its feeling of power breaks the link to actual increase of power, then it also dissolves any necessary connection between the human will to power and hostile forms of exercise of power over others" (2001: 108). The feeling of power can be acquired through the domination of others but it can equally be acquired through compassion towards others, through the disciplining of oneself and so on, depending on the ethical perspective in terms of which human beings experience their activity (*ibid.*: 109).[15]

Conceptualized thus, the principle of will to power provides Nietzsche with a general hypothesis in terms of which to account for the widely varying forms of human behaviour as governed by an architectonic interest in the feeling of power. The continuity between the motivation for the Christian re-evaluation of the values of antiquity and for Nietzsche's proposed re-evaluation of Christian values is, thus, that both are to be understood as expressions of will to power.

IV

But what of Nietzsche's need of criteria for evaluating moral perspectives? This issue also turns on Nietzsche's stress on the point that the feeling of power need have no necessary connection to power. The criterion of evaluation that Nietzsche proposes is whether the feeling of power expresses and tracks power, where this criterion can be taken to be well grounded just in so far as the principle of will to power provides a compelling explanation of human behaviour. The argument runs thus:

1. *if* one accepts the principle of will to power as a principle of explanation, then
2. one has accepted that human beings are characterized by an architectonic interest in the self-reflexive experience of power, and
3. since it is a necessary condition of the self-reflexive experience of power that the feeling of power is taken to express power, then
4. one must also accept that moral perspectives and the valuations of which they are composed can be evaluated in terms of whether (the degree of) the feeling of power that human beings experience under a given moral perspective expresses and tracks (their degree of) power.

Hence, the crucial question is this: under what conditions does the feeling of power *necessarily* express and track power?

To get clear about this topic, it is absolutely vital to recognize that, that in the case of human beings, for Nietzsche, "power" is a synonym of "agency". This point is made plain by Nietzsche's identification of will to power with "the instinct for freedom"; power, in Nietzsche's lexicon, simply is free agency (GM II §18). Consequently, the argument stated above can be rewritten thus:

1. *If* one accepts the principle of will to power as a principle of explanation, then
2. one has accepted that human beings are characterized by an architectonic interest in the self-reflexive experience of agency, and
3. since it is a necessary condition of the self-reflexive experience of agency that the feeling of agency is taken to express agency, then
4. one must also accept that moral perspectives and the valuations of which they are composed can be evaluated in terms of whether (the degree of) the feeling of agency that human beings experience under a given moral perspective expresses and tracks (their degree of) agency.

So now the crucial question is this: under what conditions does the feeling of agency necessarily express and track agency?

At this stage, one might worry that Nietzsche's criterion is no criterion at all since, to put it over-simply, if one is committed to the traditional philosophical doctrine of free will, one will tend to the thought that the feeling of agency always expresses agency and, if one is a traditional determinist, one will argue that the feeling of agency never expresses agency. However, Nietzsche rejects the metaphysical picture against the background of which the free will versus determinism debate is the only intelligible way of conceiving of ourselves; indeed, he regards this picture as motivated by a specific kind of moral disposition that is focused on the issue of *blame* (and in the *Genealogy* he will present an account of how we acquire this metaphysical picture; see e.g. BGE §21).[16] Borrowing Gemes's terms, we can say that in opposition to this picture in which the contrast between freedom and unfreedom is characterized as the contrast between *deserts* free will and determinism, Nietzsche proposes a picture in which the contrast is that between *agency* free will and mere doings. For Nietzsche, as Gemes puts it, "the free will debate is intrinsically tied to the question of agency; what constitutes an action as opposed to a mere doing?" Viewed from this stance, it is immediately apparent how the feeling of agency might fail to express agency since if one is held captive by a (mistaken) picture of agency such as that of "deserts free will", then one will experience the feeling of agency as a product of mere doings because one will (mis)identify mere doings as actions.[17] This point is essential if one is to recognize the force of Nietzsche's use of the concept of *degeneration* in *Beyond Good and Evil* (which foreshadows his discussion of *decadence* in the post-*Genealogy* works). This concept refers to a condition in which the enhancement of the *feeling of agency* experienced by human beings who understand themselves in terms of *"the morality of herd animals"* (which Nietzsche takes to be characteristic of modern Europe) expresses the diminution, rather than enhancement, of *agency* (BGE §§202–3).[18] Hence Nietzsche's contention that modern man sees himself as *higher man*, as the meaning and goal of history (GM I §11), and yet represents "a stunted, almost ridiculous type, a herd animal, something well-meaning, sickly, and mediocre ...: the European of today" (BGE §62).

But while this makes clear the sense in which Nietzsche's criterion can act as a criterion, it does not yet help to specify the substantive character of this criterion since we have not yet addressed his account of the distinction between agency free will and unfreedom, between actions and mere doings.

A fairly straightforward route into this topic is provided by Nietzsche's account of agency free will in terms of a certain kind of psychological relationship to self that he often glosses as *becoming what you are* (see e.g. GS §270) or, as he later writes in *Twilight of the Idols*, "Having the will to be responsible to oneself" (TI "Expeditions of an Untimely Man" §38). Nietzsche's claim then is that the feeling of power/agency only necessarily expresses and tracks power/agency in so far as the agent stands in this kind of relationship to himself or, rather, that it is only in standing in this type of relationship to himself that the individual is constituted as an agent, as a being whose doings are actions. As we shall see, this account is closely related to his reasons for deploying the deliberately provocative use of the notions of *herd* and *herd-morality* in his depictions of his modern human beings and the Christian moral inheritance that he takes to characterize them. The basic thought here is that freedom can be seen under two aspects.

Under the first aspect, freedom requires that we are entitled to regard our intentions, values, beliefs and so on, as our *own*,[19] where a condition of being so entitled is that the intentions, beliefs, values and so on that we express in acting are self-determined. Nietzsche, in common with other advocates of an expressivist understanding of agency for whom *"Das Thun is alles"* (The deed is everything) (GM I §13),[20] takes the relationship of an artist to his work as exemplifying the appropriate kind of self-relation. It is (i) one in which one's actions are expressive of one's intentions where this means that one's intention-in-acting is not prior to its expression but rather is realized as such only in being adequately expressed (the work is *his* to the degree that it adequately expresses his intentions and his intentions become choate as *his* intentions only through their adequate expression)[21] and (ii) one's activity appeals to no authority independent of, or external to, the norms that govern the practice in which one is engaged. This is the background against which we can grasp the point of Nietzsche's recourse to stressing the first-person pronoun in talk of *"my* truths" (BGE §232) and assertions such as "My judgment is *my* judgment, no one else is easily entitled to it" (BGE §43) as well as his claim in arguing:

> A virtue must be *our* invention, *our* most personal need and self-defense; a virtue in any other sense is merely a danger. What is not a condition of our life *harms* it: a virtue that stems purely from a feeling of respect for the concept "virtue", as Kant would have it, is harmful. "Virtue", "duty", "the good in itself", the good with the character of impersonality and universal validity – all phantasms in which the decline and final exhaustion of life, the Königsberg Chineseness, expresses

itself. The most basic laws of self-preservation and growth demand the opposite: that everyone invents *his own* virtue, *his own* categorical imperative.

(A §11; cf. Guay 2002: 310–11)

Under the second aspect, freedom requires that we engage in critically distanced reflection on our current self-understanding. Nietzsche's point is that freedom demands:

the ability to take one's virtues and oneself as objects of reflection, assessment and possible transformation, so that one can determine who one is … As Nietzsche pointed out "whoever reaches his ideal in doing so transcends it". To take ourselves as potentially free requires that we are not merely bearers of good qualities but self-determining beings capable of distanced reflection. So to attain one's ideal is always that and also to attain a new standpoint, from which one can look beyond it to how to live one's life in the future.

(Guay 2002: 315)

It is just such a process that Nietzsche sought to give expression in "Schopenhauer as Educator".[22] Notice that the thought expressed here is analogous to the thought that the artist in having completed a work that adequately expresses his intentions takes that work as an object of critical reflection and assessment, and so moves on to tackle new tasks, to take up new challenges. In the light of this concept of freedom, we can see the point of Nietzsche's talk of the *herd* as referring to (and seeking to provoke a certain self-contempt in) those who fail to live up to the demands of freedom. This is grounded in his characterization of *herd-morality* as a form of morality that obstructs the realization of freedom by, on the one hand, construing agency in non-expressive terms such that the feeling of agency has no necessary relationship to agency – and, on the other hand, presenting moral rules as unconditional (in virtue of their source in an extra-human authority) and, hence, as beyond critical reflection and assessment. Herd-morality, to return to the artistic analogy, is characterized by a relationship to one's work in which (i) one treats "the medium through which its work is to be done as a mere vehicle for the thought or feeling it is attempting to clarify" (Ridley 1998b: 36) and (ii) takes the standards according to which a work is to be judged as external to the artistic tradition.[23] The salience of this discussion for our consideration of Nietzsche's criterion of evaluation is that the feeling of agency expresses agency just in so far as the values according to which we act are our *own*, are self-determined, that is, are constraints that we reflectively endorse as conditions of our agency.[24]

We should note further that this account of freedom serves to provide Nietzsche with the resources needed to address two issues raised earlier. First, it answers Dostoevsky's worry about moral agency *per se* following the death of God in that it makes freedom the basis on which ethical norms are constituted as binding. Secondly, it responds to the point expressed by Nietzsche in *Daybreak*, namely, that he could see no non-circular way of positing a substantive universal moral ideal for humanity in that by grounding ethical agency in his decidedly non-metaphysical account of freedom, Nietzsche accommodates the thought that philosophy cannot legislate a substantive universal moral ideal *within* his account of agency free will.

V

Yet the proposal of this criterion of evaluation may seem simply to move the problem of authority back one step. Will to power (and the account of freedom that goes along with it) is, it may be pointed out, simply part of Nietzsche's perspective; the fact that the doctrine of will to power provides Nietzsche with a way of accounting for perspectives (including his own) and, indeed, for perspectivism, does not imply – incoherently – that it has a non-perspectival status, but merely that it is an integral element in Nietzsche's efforts to develop a perspective that is maximally coherent.[25] But if will to power is part of Nietzsche's perspective, a perspective oriented to translating man back into nature, then what authority can it have for those who do not share this perspective? To see how Nietzsche addresses this issue, we need to sketch out his perspectivism in more detail than the hitherto rather fleeting references to perspectives have done.

In common with a number of other contemporary commentators on Nietzsche's perspectivism,[26] I take this doctrine to offer "a *deflationary* view of the nature of justification: there is no coherent notion of justification other than ratification in the terms provided by one's perspective" (Reginster 2000: 40). Nietzsche does not say very much about perspectives or the individuation of perspectives[27] but we can discern from his examples that Nietzsche's concept of a perspective, like Wittgenstein's concept of a picture, refers to a system of judgements, where "this system is not a more or less arbitrary and doubtful point of departure for all our arguments: no, it belongs to the essence of what we call an argument. The system is not so much the point of departure, as the element in which arguments have their life" (Wittgenstein 1975: §105).[28] A perspective as a system of judgements denotes the space of reasons "which constitute an agent's *deliberative viewpoint*, i.e., the viewpoint from which he forms his all-things-considered judgments about what to do" (Reginster 2000: 43).[29] In endorsing this stance, Nietzsche thus confronts the very issue raised with respect to will to power in its most acute form, namely, how he can justify the authority of his perspective. What Nietzsche needs here is a way of showing those committed to holding another perspective that they should endorse his perspective in the light of reasons internal to their current perspective. Moreover, since (as we have seen) Nietzsche also holds that reasons motivate only in so far as they appeal to values that are part of the motivational set of those to whom the reasons are addressed, then, for his argument to be effective, the reasons that he adduces must express values intrinsic to the perspective currently held by those he is concerned to persuade.

What Nietzsche needs, it seems, is an argument with the following form: in so far as you are committed to perspective A, then reasons x and y provide you with grounds to acknowledge the superiority of perspective B in terms of value z, where z is an intrinsic (i.e. independently motivating) value in perspective A.[30] But although an argument of this type looks sufficient for the kind of internal criticism needed in that it provides independently motivating reasons to move from perspective A to perspective B, it is not sufficient for this move to be reflectively stable. The problem is this: if it is the case that we are motivated to move from perspective A to perspective B in terms that appeal to value z, then if value z is not an intrinsic value in perspective B, we find ourselves in the position of reflectively endorsing perspective B on the basis of a value that is not an intrinsic value within this perspective, that is, for reasons that do not count as the appropriate (i.e. independently motivating) kind of reasons (if, indeed, they count as reasons at all) within this perspective.[31] Consequently, if our reasons for endorsing perspective B are to stand in the right kind of motivational relationship to both perspective A and perspective B, the value to which these reasons appeal must be an intrinsic value not only in perspective A but also perspective B. The implication of these reflections is that Nietzsche's claims concerning perspectivism, will to power and freedom have authority for us only in so far as we are provided with reasons that are authoritative-for-us, given our existing perspective, and stand in the right kind of motivational relationship to both our existing perspective and Nietzsche's perspective. If the project of re-evaluation is to be coherent, Nietzsche needs to supply an argument that does this work.

Conclusion

Nietzsche's reflections on the problems with his initial view of the character and requirements of the project of re-evaluation in *Daybreak* have led to very significant extensions, developments and refinements of his understanding of this project and its demands. There are three principal demands that Nietzsche now takes this project to involve. First, consequent to his development of the view of Christianity as a perspective expressing a taste for the unconditional, Nietzsche needs an account of how we have become subject to this taste and held captive by this perspective. Secondly, consequent to his development of the view of our will to truth as internal to the Christian perspective, Nietzsche needs an account of how the will to truth develops that explains how it is possible for us to free ourselves from the grip of the Christian perspective and the taste for the unconditional that it expresses and why we ought to disavow this taste. Thirdly, consequent to his development of, and commitment to, the doctrines of will to power and of perspectivism, Nietzsche needs to develop the account demanded by the first and second requirements in naturalistic terms and such that it secures the authority of Nietzsche's perspective in a reflectively stable manner. It is the necessity of meeting these demands that motivates Nietzsche's development of genealogy as a mode of enquiry, and if Nietzsche can meet these demands in his genealogy of morality it will provide compelling reasons for those subject to the peculiar perspective of "morality" to acknowledge the need for a re-evaluation of values by showing them that "morality" involves a fundamental misunderstanding of ourselves as ethical agents. Hence the point of the following remark from the preface to the *Genealogy*:

> Previously, no one had expressed even the remotest doubt or shown the slightest hesitation in assuming the "good man" to be of greater worth than the "evil man", of greater worth in his usefulness in promoting the progress of human *existence* (including the future of man). What? What if there existed a

symptom of regression in the "good man", likewise, a danger, a temptation, a poison, a narcotic, by means of which the present were living *at the expense of the future*? ... So that none other than morality itself would be the culprit, if the *highest power and splendour* of the human type, in itself a possibility, were never to be reached? So that morality would constitute the danger of dangers? (GM Preface §6)

It is just this case that the *Genealogy* will attempt to establish.

CHAPTER THREE

Rhetoric and re-evaluation

It is, I contend, a feature of Nietzsche's commitment to the philosophical ideal of reflectiveness that his work does not limit itself to seeking to offer cogent philosophical argument for a given claim, but also, and further, considers how to give expression to these arguments in a way that will most persuasively engage his audience. This is not least because of the central role that Nietzsche's account from *Daybreak* onwards assigns to the affects. An implication of this commitment to what is perhaps the most central ideal of the philosophical tradition is that if the argument proposed thus far is cogent, we would expect to see signs of these shifts in the development of Nietzsche's rhetorical strategies. While in this section I cannot undertake a full analysis of the shifts in Nietzsche's rhetoric during this period, I will attempt to adduce evidence in support of the claims advanced thus far by focusing on, first, the shift in strategy from *Human, All Too Human* to *Daybreak*, in which I have argued that the movement from the devaluation to the re-evaluation of "morality" is accomplished and, secondly, the shift from *Daybreak* to *The Gay Science*, in which I have claimed that Nietzsche comes to discern the problem of *not inferring*. To the extent that the developments in Nietzsche's rhetorical strategies are explicable as being motivated by these shifts in his philosophical stance, this will support not only the account I have offered but also my contention that the complexity of Nietzsche's work – perhaps particularly the *Genealogy* – does not betray a lack of analytical rigour but, on the contrary, a deep commitment to the philosophical ideal of reflectiveness.

I

In *Human, All Too Human*, Nietzsche's understanding is that his critical task with respect to religion and metaphysics is to undermine their attraction. However, he does not take his success to depend on convincing his readers that he has demonstrated the methodological failings of metaphysics and the irrelevance of the existence of a metaphysical world. It is, he argues, sufficient for his purposes to have cultivated a sceptical attitude towards metaphysics since, in practical terms, this has the same effect as a refutation, namely, a mistrust of metaphysical claims (HAH I §21). Whether this disavowal of metaphysics takes *de jure* or *de facto* forms is of little moment to Nietzsche because his criticism of metaphysics is directed to practical ends, namely, to weaken and, finally, eliminate the *needs* that metaphysics and religion (as the popular expression of metaphysics) have satisfied (HAH I §§27 and 108). He takes up this task by exposing the falsity of the beliefs that sustain these needs and, in so doing, understands himself to be supporting the movement of culture from a religious to a scientific viewpoint. In other words, Nietzsche's position in *Human, All Too Human*, like that of those other "masters of suspicion" Marx and Freud, is that of the Enlightenment figure of the ideology critic concerned to provide a critical account (combining genetic and epistemological reflections) of the psychological bases on which human beings come to hold to the illusions expressed by religious and metaphysical beliefs; such a critical account will, on this view, produce a process of self-reflection in virtue of which those subject to the ideology in question will be liberated from these false beliefs. Thus, for example, Nietzsche writes:

> a certain false psychology, a certain kind of fantasy in the interpretation of motives and experiences is the necessary presupposition for becoming a Christian and for feeling the need for redemption. With the insight into this aberration of reason and imagination, one ceases to be a Christian.
>
> (HAH §135)

By demonstrating both the non-rational causes of such beliefs and the illusory status of these beliefs (i.e. their incompatibility with our best epistemic standards), Nietzsche can reasonably hold himself to be contributing to "the tremendous task facing the great spirits of the coming century" (HAH §25). In rhetorical terms, this finds expression in both the cool distance of Nietzsche's tone, which led Erwin

Rodhe to characterize coming to this work from Nietzsche's previous writings in terms of "being chased from the *calidarium*, the steamy waters, immediately into an icy *frigidarium*" (cited in Heller 1986: xi), and the composition of volume I of *Human, All Too Human*, in which the impartial spectatorial eye constructed in the opening section of the work "Of First and Last Things" casts its sceptical gaze in turn over morality, religion and art: the domains whose higher value is explained by recourse to a metaphysical realm. Nietzsche's cultivation of this tone is not merely designed to cultivate a sceptical distance towards metaphysics in his audience; it is also intended to exemplify a stance towards the world that addresses the issue of how to live with the destructive scepticism that his work exhibits. Nietzsche is all too aware that if, as he argues, the naturalistic cast of mind brings with it an acknowledgment that every "belief in the value and dignity of life rests on false thinking" (HAH I §33), the following problem becomes pressing:

> But will our philosophy not thus become a tragedy? Will truth not become inimical to life, to the better man? A question seems to lie heavily on our tongue and yet refuses to be uttered: whether one *could* consciously reside in untruth? Or, if one were *obliged* to, whether death would not be preferable? For there is no longer any "ought"; for morality, insofar as it was an "ought", has been just as much annihilated by our mode of thinking as has religion. Knowledge can allow as motives only pleasure and pain, utility and injury: but how will these motives come to terms with the sense for truth? For they are in contact with errors (insofar as inclination and aversion, and their very unjust assessments are, as we said, the essential determinants of pleasure and pain). The whole of human life is sunk deeply in untruth; the individual cannot draw it up out of this well without thereby growing profoundly disillusioned about his own past, without finding his present motives, such as that of honour, absurd, and pouring mockery and contempt on the passions which reach out to the future and promise happiness in it. Is it true, is all that remains a mode of thought whose outcome on a personal level is despair and on a theoretical level a philosophy of destruction? (HAH I §34)

Nietzsche's response is to suggest that this need not be true to the extent that we cultivate the stance of the disinterested spectator who does not engage in value-judgements but simply enjoys the spectacle of life: "In the end one would live among men and with oneself as in *nature*, without praising, blaming, contending, gazing contentedly, as though at a spectacle, upon many things for which one formerly felt only fear" (*ibid.*). It is just such a stance that Nietzsche's rhetoric in this work is designed to exemplify and elicit, and it is hard not to see this stance as significantly continuous with Schopenhauer's image of the man who has escaped willing and desire.

The nature of the demands on Nietzsche's rhetorical abilities changes as he comes to his initial formulation of the project of re-evaluation in *Daybreak*. In *Human, All Too Human*, Nietzsche had directed his rhetorical powers to the problem of living with the consequences of the destructive scepticism that his position unleashed and had taken his persuasive task to consist in simply providing reasons to be sceptical with respect to the metaphysical foundations of value and, hence, religious, moral and aesthetic beliefs. However, in *Daybreak*, Nietzsche sees the major issue of persuasion confronting the newly developed project of re-evaluation to be the fact that although a system of moral feelings is a product of a system of moral judgements (D §38), it is our moral feelings, rather than our moral beliefs, that are the proximal causes of our moral actions and reactions – and that our system of moral feelings can persist in the absence of the system of beliefs that gave rise to this affective structuring of our drives (D §99).[1] Hence, Nietzsche adopts the rhetorical tactic of stressing as negative those features of Christianity that he takes to have the least grip on his audience, for example Christianity's "*diabolising* of Eros":

> All our thinking and poeticising, from the highest to the lowest, is characterised, and more than characterised, by the excessive importance attached to the love story: on this account it may be that posterity will judge the whole inheritance of Christian culture to be marked by something crack-brained and petty. (D §76)

Similarly, Nietzsche's frequent appeal – as in this passage – to the judgement of the present by the future not only marks his hope that we shall overcome our Christian second nature but also expresses a rhetorical strategy designed to elicit a distancing effect with respect to this second nature in his audience by presenting it as something that will be judged in the future to be laughable: a tactic that plays off the very sense of pride that Nietzsche discerns in his audience. This tactic

– Nietzsche's most general rhetorical tactic throughout *Daybreak* – is informed by his sense that pride is both the major obstacle to the emergence of a post-Christian ethical sensibility and that this pridefulness can be used to undermine its own obstructive effects:

> *The brake.* – To suffer for the sake of morality and then to be told that this kind of suffering is founded on an *error*; this arouses indignation. For there is a unique consolation in affirming through one's suffering a "profounder world of truth" than any other world is, and one would much *rather* suffer and thereby feel oneself *exalted* above reality ... than be without suffering but also without this feeling that one is exalted. It is thus pride, and the customary manner in which pride is gratified, which stands in the way of a new *understanding* of morality. What force, therefore, will have to be employed if this brake is to be removed? More pride? A new pride? (D §32)

Although Nietzsche's responses are themselves addressed to the reader in interrogative mode, it is clear enough from his practice that this use of pride against its own obstructive effects is central to the work that *Daybreak* seeks to accomplish. For example, Nietzsche exploits his audience's pride in their own autonomy to his ends in passages such as the following:

> *Feelings and their origination in judgments.* – "Trust your feelings!" – But feelings are nothing final or original; behind feelings there stand judgments and evaluations which we inherit in the form of feelings (inclinations, aversions). The inspiration born of a feeling is the grandchild of a judgment – and often of a false judgment! – and in any event not a child of your own! To trust one's feelings – means to give more obedience to one's grandfather and grandmother and their grandparents than to the gods which are in *us*: our reason and our experience. (D §35)

Thus, Nietzsche's rhetorical strategy shifts to accommodate the fact that he now sees that the persuasive problem posed for his project of re-evaluation is that our relationship to our moral values is not simply an epistemic issue but also, and in some respects more basically, an affective one.

II

We can track a similar shift as Nietzsche comes to acknowledge that the persuasive problem confronting the project of re-evaluation goes deeper with his recognition that (Christian) morality is a perspective in whose grip we are held. Here I shall focus on Nietzsche's attempt to give expression to this problem in "The Madman (*Der tolle Mensch*)" in *The Gay Science* (§125): in which, I shall argue, we see Nietzsche attempting to give expression to the problem that confronts his project: what I have described as the problem of *not inferring*.

The passage runs as follows:

> *The madman.* – Have you not heard of that madman who lit a lantern in the bright morning hours, ran to the market place, and cried incessantly: "I seek God! I seek God!" – As many of those who did not believe in God were standing around just then, he provoked much laughter. Has he got lost? asked one. Did he lose his way like a child? asked another. Or is he hiding? Is he afraid of us? Has he gone on a voyage? Emigrated? – Thus they yelled and laughed.
>
> The madman jumped into their midst and pierced them with his eyes. "Whither is God?" he cried; "I will tell you. *We have killed him* – you and I. All of us are his murderers. But how did we do this? How could we drink up the sea? Who gave us the sponge to wipe away the entire horizon? What were we doing when we unchained this earth from its sun? Whither is it moving now? Whither are we moving? Away from all suns? Are we not plunging continually? Backward, sideward, forward, in all directions? Is there still any up or down? Are we not straying as through an empty space? Do we not feel the breath of empty space? Has it not become colder? Is not night continually closing in on us? Do we not need to light lanterns in the morning? Do we hear nothing as yet of the noise of the gravediggers who are burying God? Do we smell nothing as yet of the divine decomposition? Gods, too, decompose. God is dead. God remains dead. And we have killed him.
>
> "How shall we comfort ourselves, the murderers of all murderers? What was holiest and mightiest of all that the world has yet owned has bled to death under our knives: who will wipe this blood off us? What water is there for us to clean

ourselves? What festivals of atonement, what sacred games shall we have to invent? Is not the greatness of this deed simply too great for us? Must we not ourselves become gods simply to appear worthy of it? There has never been a greater deed; and whoever is born after us – for the sake of this deed he will belong to a higher history than all history hitherto."

Here, the madman fell silent and looked at his listeners; and they, too, were silent and stared at him in astonishment. At last he threw his lantern on the ground, and it broke into pieces and went out. "I have come too early," he said then; "my time is not yet. This tremendous event is still on its way, still wandering; it has not yet reached the ears of men. Lightning and thunder require time; the light of stars requires time; deeds, though done, still require time to be seen and heard. This deed is still more distant from then than the most distant stars – *and yet they have done it themselves.*"

It has been related further that on the same day the madman forced his way into several churches and there struck up his *requiem aeternam deo.* Led out and called to account, he is said always to have replied nothing but: "What after all are these churches now if they are not the tombs and sepulchers of God?" (GS §125)[2]

Recounted as a piece of news from the marketplace by an anonymous narrator who characterizes the central character of the parable as a madman (in the colloquial rather than clinical sense), the story divides fairly readily into four stages:

1. A man ("the madman"), carrying a lantern without any practical reason to do so, proclaims to those people present in the marketplace that he seeks God. Not believing in God, they mock him.
2. He turns on them and delivers a speech on the death and decomposition of God, but this is greeted with silence.
3. The man smashes his redundant lantern, announcing that he is too early; his audience are not yet ready for his words because the event of which he speaks, although it has happened, has not yet arrived.
4. Later this man forces his way into churches to sing a requiem for God and justifies his action to those who question him by asking what churches are now if not monuments of the dead God.

51

At the heart of this parable is a failure of communication and an explanation of this failure, and we shall focus closely on these elements, but bracketing this failure and explanation of failure are the opening and closing passages, which, I suggest, are crucial to an understanding of how the central passages relate to Nietzsche's philosophical project.

The first point to note is that this parable ties the figure of the madman to the ancient Cynic philosopher Diogenes of Sinope, otherwise known as Diogenes the Dog (Niehues-Pröbsting 1996). The opening passage explicitly echoes a story concerning this Cynic philosopher recounted in Diogenes Laertius's *Lives of the Eminent Philosophers*:[3] "He lit a lamp in broad daylight and said, as he went about, 'I am looking for a man [anthropon]'" (Laertius 1932: VI 40–42).

As Niehues-Pröbsting comments: "In a grandiose gesture, intensifying the Cynic's critique of morals into an enlightened critique of religion, Nietzsche made the popular anecdote of Diogenes with the lantern into the literary frame and expression of one of his central thoughts" (1996: 361). The closing passage is not as explicit in its reference but, since an infamous feature of Diogenes' exemplification of his teaching in his life was to flout social conventions that he held to be "unnatural" by, for example, masturbating in the marketplace, before offering frank responses on being held to account (Laertius 1932: VI 21–81), it does not seem unreasonable to suggest that the madman's brazen activity of singing a requiem for God in several churches (and his frank response on being called to account) deliberately exhibits the spirit of this Cynic philosopher.[4] Niehues-Pröbsting is again to the point:

> Even the description of this enlightening figure as a madman can be traced back to the Cynic tradition. For it was typical of the Cynic, particularly as depicted by Diogenes Laertius, that on the one hand he caused laughter by means of his humour and satire, but on the other hand was declared mad because of his paradoxical, exalted and shameless behaviour. Nietzsche made his ironic-satirical enlightener undergo the same treatment: he is laughed at. The people around him answer with irony, and when the madman becomes serious, they react with consternation. (1996: 362)

It may be worth noting in this context that Nietzsche's relationship to the figure of Diogenes had already been made explicit in *Human, All Too Human* when, under the title "The Modern Diogenes", he wrote:

"Before one searches for man, one must have found a lantern. – Will it have to be the *Cynic's* lantern?" (WS §18).

Given that Nietzsche has provided us with this reference as a clue to the interpretation of this parable, what should we make of it? Consider the following related reports concerning Diogenes' teaching:

> One day he shouted out for men, and when people collected, hit out at them with his stick, saying "It was men I called for, not scoundrels ...."
>
> ... As he was leaving the public baths, somebody inquired if many men were bathing. He said, No. But to another who asked if there was a great crowd of bathers, he said, Yes.
>
> (Laertius 1932: VI 32–42)

Two points are worth noting about this teaching strategy. First, Diogenes is prepared to risk being thought a fool or madman in order to accomplish his teaching. One can all too easily imagine a spectator describing Diogenes' activity under the title *Der tolle Mensch*; indeed the Sophist philosopher Dio Chryostom points out that this was one of the standard responses to Diogenes' performances in the *chreia* tradition (Branham 1996: 102). Secondly, this teaching does not consist in supplying new beliefs but in seeking to reorient his audience's relationship to themselves and what matters to them; not least through the example of his own life, Diogenes is trying to bring his audience to a recognition of the ethically problematic character of their existing way of life and the need for a re-evaluation of their values.[5] With these two points to orient us, let us return to Nietzsche's parable.

Since the madman knows as well as his mocking audience that God is dead, his entrance into the marketplace carrying a lamp and crying "I seek God!" is designed, following the practice of Diogenes, to elicit the attention and, no doubt, also the mockery of the audience of atheists who greet him in order to provide an occasion for his excoriating funeral oration. In so doing he is certainly charging his audience with acknowledging their relationship to the death of God, but he is doing so deliberately as one seeking to enlighten; consequently, when his speech is greeted by astonished silence, it should not surprise us that he attempts both to account for his failure and to develop a new strategy of enlightenment since this is just what is required of one who is seriously engaged in the activity of enlightenment, that is, one who is willing even to act as a "crazy man" in order to enlighten. If his speech leaves the people in the marketplace unmoved, and if it does so because his audience is not yet ready for his message, then perhaps all that he can do is attempt to cultivate the conditions under which they may become ready for this message. This is, I take it, the point of the activity reported in the final passage of *The Gay Science* §125. Following the example of Diogenes once more, the madman flouts polite social convention and forces his way into several churches, strikes up his *requiem aeternam deo* and, crucially, when called to account offers a reason that his audience of atheists cannot deny: "What after all are these churches now if they are not the tombs and sepulchres of God?" Since it is common ground between the madman and his audience that belief in the Christian god has become unbelievable, by offering this reason the madman calls on his audience to reflect honestly on what it is to acknowledge the death of God; what sense does it make, he asks them, to call to account someone whose actions simply express frankly what any individual of intellectual integrity admits – God is dead?

The claim, then, is that *The Gay Science* §125 presents a parable of (a failure of) enlightenment, and this claim is further supported by attending not simply to the initial appearance of the lamp as referring us to Diogenes, but also to its second and third appearances. The second appearance – "Do we not need to light lanterns in the morning?" – occurs in the madman's peroration on the death and decomposition of God in the course of a series of rhetorical questions that pose the issue of the death of God in terms of *disorientation*: a disorientation of our physical body in the world that illustrates the disorientation of our ethical being in the world. This "disorientation in thinking", as one might put it, reveals by analogy – "Is there still any up or down?" – the depth that the madman ascribes to the impact of the death of God on our ethical being in the world. Here we can say that the madman is taking with utter seriousness Kant's recognition that the intelligibility of moral behaviour (of that particular form – and local type – of moral reasoning that Kant identifies as morality as such) requires the *res fidei*: God, immortality and freedom. The precision of this second reference is that it continues the analogy of physical disorientation but also calls for an enlightening of the Enlightenment. If the daybreak of the urbane atheists gathered in the marketplace – the cockcrow of positivism – represents the first wave of enlightenment, then the madman's rhetorical question registers the need of these first-wave enlighteners for further enlightenment. Indeed, precisely to the degree that the first enlightenment succeeds, it renders us vulnerable to the disorientation of thinking of which the madman speaks and, consequently, in need of re-orientation (or, let us say, re-evaluation). However, prior to any such re-orientation, there must be the recognition of the need for re-orientation, and it is the failure of such recognition to appear that is symbolized by the third appearance of the lantern of enlightenment: the madman's smashing of the lantern on the floor. The madman has moved his audience from the comfort of laughter to an astonished state of silence – and this is not nothing – but he has not elicited the response of recognition of the need for re-orientation that he sought and seeks. His activity as *Aufklärer* is a failure: a failure that, as *Aufklärer*, the madman is constrained to explain.

Let us turn then to this failure and the madman's explanation of it. To do so we need to begin by returning to the question of what the madman is seeking to teach. Consider again the level of the analogies deployed by the madman in figuring the death of God as spatial disorientation:

> Who gave us the sponge to wipe away the entire horizon? What were we doing when we unchained this earth from its sun? Whither is it moving now? Whither are we moving? Away from all suns? Are we not plunging continually? Backward, sideward, forward, in all directions? Is there still any up or down? Are we not straying as through an empty space? Do we not feel the breath of empty space? Has it not become colder? Is not night continually closing in on us?
>
> (GS §125)

Taken literally, these questions ask us to consider ourselves positioned in an empty space, a space with no markers, signposts, orientation points; unchaining the earth from the sun, we have moved to new spaces that leave us unable to position ourselves by reference to the sun – we have shifted into *the horizon of the infinite*. As Nietzsche puts it:

> We have left the land and have embarked. We have burned our bridges behind us – indeed, we have gone further and destroyed the land behind us. ... Woe, when you feel homesick for the land as if it had offered more *freedom* – and there is no longer any "land".
>
> (GS §124)

We can make sense of these analogies by recalling the opening sections of Book III cited in the earlier discussion of the problem of *not*

55

inferring, in which Nietzsche made the point that the death of God extends into the warp and weft of our lives; the Christian system of judgements, its way of valuing, is deeply woven into the fabric of our culture. Understood in this way, the death of God has implications, the depth and extent of which are as yet uncharted, for our system of judgements as a whole, which is to say, for our form of life, our ways of being in the world. Thus, for example, Nietzsche notes that among the effects of Christianity has been the cultivation of a particular picture of the will that persists despite our loss of belief in Christianity (GS §127).

In support of this reading of the madman's first speech, we can note Nietzsche's remarks when he returns in 1887 to add a fifth book to *The Gay Science* and in its opening section writes of the death of God: "how much must collapse now that this faith has been undermined because it was built upon this faith, propped up by it, grown into it: for example, the whole of our European morality" (GS §343). This remark is situated within a repetition, this time voiced by Nietzsche, of the madman's account of his failure to communicate the meaning of the death of God to his audience and so directs us to what I will suggest is the second point in favour of this reading, namely, that it provides a plausible account of the madman's explanation of his failure. In *The Gay Science*, the relevant passage reads as follows:

> Here, the madman fell silent and looked at his listeners; and they, too, were silent and stared at him in astonishment. At last he threw his lantern on the ground, and it broke into pieces and went out. "I have come too early," he said then; "my time is not yet. This tremendous event is still on its way, still wandering; it has not yet reached the ears of men. Lightning and thunder require time; the light of stars requires time; deeds, though done, still require time to be seen and heard. This deed is still more distant from then than the most distant stars – *and yet they have done it themselves*." (GS §125)

Later in *The Gay Science*, the point is presented thus:

> But in the main one may say: The event [that "God is dead"] is far too great, too distant, too remote from the multitude's capacity for comprehension even for the tidings of it to be thought of as having *arrived* as yet. Much less may one suppose that many people know as yet *what* this event really

56

means – and how much must collapse now that this faith has
been undermined .... (GS §343)

An important clue as to the interpretation of this claim that the "greatest recent event" has happened and yet has still to arrive is given when
Nietzsche writes:

> Even we born guessers of riddles who are, as it were, wait-
> ing on the mountains, posted between today and tomorrow,
> stretched in the contradiction between today and tomorrow,
> we firstlings and premature births of the coming century, to
> whom the shadows [cast by the death of God] that must soon
> envelop Europe really *should* have appeared by now – why
> is it that even we look forward to the approaching gloom
> without any real sense of involvement and above all without
> any worry and fear for *ourselves*? Are we perhaps still too
> much under the impression of the *initial consequences* of this
> event ... (*Ibid.*)

The salient feature of this passage is its hint that the "as yet not arrived"
character of the death of God is linked to the lack of a "real sense of
involvement" with this event. Randall Havas gets the significance of
this point right, without noticing its relationship to the character of
Diogenes' pedagogy, when he comments:

> The people to whom [the madman] announces the death of
> God are, in effect, unwilling to let that event matter to them,
> to count it *as* an event. Overcoming such resistance would be
> a matter of a shift in their relationship to the madman, but it
> would not involve any further beliefs about what he actually
> says. (Havas 1995: 177)

In the terms that I have adopted, we may say that the audience's
avoidance of the meaning of the death of God (as the disorientation
of thinking) is this resistance to letting this event matter to them, to
counting this event as an event. However, Havas goes astray when he
continues, "Section 125 suggests that the people in the marketplace
understand well enough what the madman says; they simply cannot
see why they should care about it" (*ibid.*). On the contrary, it is the
fact that they cannot see the pointfulness of the madman's utterances
– recall their astonished silence – which marks the sense in which they

fail to understand what the madman says, a failure attested to by the designation of the madman as such. The madman's audience can follow his words, as it were, but in so far as they see no place or occasion for these words to signify, the madman's utterances remain unintelligible to them. However, the point to stress here is one on which I agree with Havas, namely, that overcoming their resistance to acknowledging the death of God does not require that the madman's audience acquire any new beliefs but rather that their relationship to the madman changes such that they become aware of what they already know. We can put it this way: in coming to see the madman's utterances as meaningful, his audience of atheists would come to see the death of God as an event that extends into the warp and weft of our ways of living, that is, to acknowledge that we abide within the terms of the decomposition of God.

We are in a position now to understand the madman's failure to enlighten his audience of atheists, an audience that thinks, as it were, that accepting a post-Christian view of the world simply entails ceasing to hold religious beliefs and accepting scientific beliefs. This failure can be stated as the subjection of the madman's teaching to a paradox of enlightenment, where it is this paradox that is dramatized in *The Gay Science* (§125): *to understand the pointfulness of the madman's speech would require that his audience are free from just that perspective from which it is the point of the madman's speech to free them.* The problem that confronts the madman is that he can only appear crazy to an audience that is enthralled by, and in thrall to, a metaphysical perspective. In this respect, *The Gay Science* (*ibid.*) sets out the condition to which Nietzsche understands his own attempt to teach the death of God to be subject. Recognizing this point accounts for the fact that Nietzsche's dramatizes this paradox (in the very specific form that he understands to apply to his own project of re-evaluation) as a parable. What Nietzsche has done in adopting this literary form as a pedagogic device is to seek to reorient our relationship to his teaching by asking us to consider this parable as a representation of our initial orientation to his teaching. By offering this parable as a puzzle for us to work through, Nietzsche can hope at least to generate in us sufficient critical distance with respect to our character as the madman's audience of enlightened atheists that we can entertain the mere possibility that we may be held captive by a perspective that obstructs our acknowledgement of the meaning of the death of God, that is, the need for a re-evaluation of values, and this is the minimum that Nietzsche needs to get his project of re-evaluation off the ground. Nietzsche's rhetorical strategy in this parable is, thus, both to acknowledge the problem of persuasion that confronts his project, that is, the need to get his audience to free themselves from the perspective to which they are currently subject, *and* to attempt to communicate this problem to his audience so that they can recognize Nietzsche's utterances in *The Gay Science* as intelligible, as potentially pointful.

Conclusion

Consideration of these shifts in Nietzsche's rhetorical strategy should, I submit, incline us both to the view that Nietzsche is acutely attentive to issues of expression and, more specifically, to the view that the development of the project of re-evaluation in the move from *Human, All Too Human* to *Daybreak* and the critical developments of the project of re-evaluation following *Daybreak* that were charted in the previous chapters have at least the right shape to account for the shifts in Nietzsche's rhetorical strategies and, in particular, the dramatization of the problem posed for his teaching by his audience's subjection to a metaphysical-cum-moral perspective. More pointedly, attending to these shifts should alert us to the fact that if we are to offer a compelling account of Nietzsche's *Genealogy*, it must be one that makes sense of the rhetorical strategies that he deploys in this work.

PART TWO

On the *Genealogy of Morality*

Introduction

Nietzsche does not claim to be the first philosopher to attempt a genealogy of morals; he does, however, claim to be the first to take up this task properly, that is with due consideration to the intrinsic requirements of this mode of enquiry.[1] Thus, commenting on Paul Rée's *The Origin of Moral Sensations*, Nietzsche writes:

> There for the first time I clearly encountered an inverted and perverted kind of genealogical hypothesis, the genuinely *English* kind, and found myself drawn to it – as opposites attract one another. ... It is possible that I have never read anything which I rejected so thoroughly, proposition by proposition, conclusion by conclusion, as this book: but without the least ill humour and impatience.   (GM Preface §4)[2]

This claim is, to put it mildly, rather self-serving in the light of Nietzsche's earlier endorsement of much of Rée's argument; however, it is true that Nietzsche has come to reject the "English" kind of genealogical argument. As he put this point in Book V of *The Gay Science*:

> These historians of morality (particularly, the Englishmen) do not amount to much: usually they themselves unsuspectingly stand under the command of a particular morality and, without knowing it, serve as its shield-bearers and followers, for example, by sharing that popular superstition of Christian Europe which people keep repeating so naively to this day, that what is characteristic of morality is selflessness, self-denial,

self-sacrifice, or sympathy and compassion. Their usual mistaken premise is that they affirm some consensus among peoples, at least among tame peoples, concerning certain moral principles, and then conclude that these principles must be unconditionally binding also for you and me – or, conversely, they see that among different peoples moral valuations are *necessarily* different and infer from this that *no* morality is binding – both of which are equally childish. The mistake of the more subtle among them is that they uncover and criticize the possibly foolish opinions of a people about their morality, or of humanity about all human morality – opinions about its origin, its religious sanction, the myth of free will and such things – and then think they have criticized the morality itself. But the value of the injunction "Thou Shalt" is still fundamentally different from and independent of such opinions about it and the weeds of error that may have overgrown it – just as surely as the value of a medication for someone sick is totally independent of whether he thinks about medicine scientifically or the way an old woman thinks about it. A morality could even have grown *out of* an error, and the realization of this fact would not so much as touch the problem of its value. Thus no one until now has examined the *value* of that most famous of all medicines called morality; and for that, one must begin by *questioning* it for once. Well then! Precisely that is our task. (GS §345)

In this specific instance, what makes the hypothesis advanced in Rée's book a genealogical hypothesis, even if of "an inverted and perverted kind", is that it attempts to provide a naturalistic account of the emergence of morality, an account that seeks to account for the origin of moral sensations in non-moral terms. What makes it "an inverted and perverted kind" of genealogical hypothesis is that Rée's account is methodologically inept with respect to the historical dimension of genealogy in that Rée seeks to account for the origin of morality in terms of the present purpose that it plays (GM I §§2–3, II §12), when it is precisely one of the achievements of Darwinian evolutionary theory to show that there need be no necessary connection between the origin of a phenomenon and its current purpose or value, a point that Nietzsche demonstrates compellingly in sections 12–14 of the second essay in respect of the phenomenon of punishment.[3] Nietzsche's criticisms of "the genuinely *English* kind" of genealogy practised by Rée indicate that his own development of genealogy – "decisive preliminary studies by a psychologist for a re-evaluation of values" (EH "Why I Write Such Good Books", on GM) directed towards "the real *history of morality*" (GM Preface §7) – will acknowledge the distinction between the conditions of emergence of the various threads that come together to compose "morality" (in the Christian perspective) and the current value of morality. Such an acknowledgement, however, raises the question of the role that Nietzsche's account of the complex and disparate conditions of emergence of the strands that compose "morality" is intended to play. Some preliminary observations on this issue will be proposed in Chapter 4, which focuses on the *Genealogy*.

The account of Nietzsche's path to genealogy in Part I claimed that the development of his philosophy between *Daybreak* and Book V of *The Gay Science* can be seen in terms of the refinement of his understanding of the demands of the project of re-evaluation with respect to the kind of argument required in both its analytical and rhetorical dimensions. Nietzsche's development of genealogy in *On the Genealogy of Morality* is, I shall suggest, precisely designed to address what Nietzsche, by the conclusion of Book V of *The Gay Science*, understands to be his target in the light of what he, at this time, understands to be the demands of the project of re-evaluation. The complex character of this task is, as the arguments of Part I indicate, composed of three demands: the need to loosen the grip on his audience of the moral perspective to which they are subject so that they can take it as an object of reflection and assessment; the need to provide arguments whose reasons can be acknowledged as such by those subject to this moral perspective (i.e. reasons that express values held to be intrinsic within this perspective); and the need to mobilize the existing affective dispositions of his audience in the service of his goal. These claims will be supported by the detailed account of the three essays composing *On the Genealogy of Morality* developed in Chapters 5–7. I conclude Part II by focusing on current debates concerning the nature of genealogical argument and addressing competing interpretations to my own.

CHAPTER FOUR

Reading the *Genealogy*

On the Genealogy of Morality is composed of a preface in which Nietzsche recounts his path to this project and three essays that take up different aspects of "morality". Mathias Risse has helpfully drawn attention to a postcard from Nietzsche to Franz Overbeck in which Nietzsche offers some elucidation with respect to the structure of this work:

> Nietzsche says that, "for the sake of clarity, it was necessary artificially to isolate the different roots of that complex structure that is called morality. Each of these three treatises expresses a single primum mobile; a fourth and fifth are missing, as is even the most essential ('the herd instinct') – for the time being, the latter had to be ignored, as too comprehensive, and the same holds for the ultimate summation of all those different elements and thus a final account of morality." Nietzsche also points out that each treatise makes a contribution to the genesis of Christianity and rejects an explanation of Christianity in terms of only one psychological category. The topics of the treatises are "good" and "evil" (first treatise), the "bad conscience" (second), and the "ascetic ideal" (third). The postcard suggests that Nietzsche discusses these topics separately because a joint treatment is too complicated, but that in reality, these ideas are inextricably intertwined, both with each other and with others that Nietzsche omits. Therefore, the three treatises should be regarded as parts of a unified theory and critique of morality. (Risse 2001: 55)

The postcard to which Risse refers suggests why Nietzsche regarded the *Genealogy* as "decisive preliminary studies by a psychologist for a re-evaluation of values" (EH "Why I Write Such Good Books", on GM) and, more significantly, indicates that we should approach the three essays as "foregrounding" different aspects of a single complex phenomenon: "morality". (This does not, however, license the view also advanced by Risse that there is no implicit narrative in the *Genealogy* – "no single historical background story in place yet" (Risse 2001: 60) – that relates the formation of the elements of "morality" treated in the three essays.) Further support for this view of the *Genealogy* is provided by Nietzsche's gloss on the three essays in *Ecce Homo*:

> Every time a beginning that is *calculated* to mislead: cool, scientific, even ironic, deliberately foreground, deliberately holding off. Gradually more unrest; sporadic lightning; very disagreeable truths are heard rumbling in the distance – until eventually a *tempo feroce* is attained in which everything rushes ahead in a tremendous tension. In the end, in the midst of perfectly gruesome detonations, a *new* truth becomes visible every time among thick clouds.
>
> The truth of the *first* inquiry is the birth of Christianity: the birth of Christianity out of the spirit of *ressentiment*, not, as people may believe, out of the "spirit" – a countermovement by its very nature, the great rebellion against the domination of *noble* values.
>
> The *second* inquiry offers the psychology of the *conscience* – which is not, as people may believe, "the voice of God in man": it is the instinct for cruelty that turns back after it can no longer discharge itself externally. Cruelty is here exposed for the first time as one of the most ancient and basic substrata of culture that simply cannot be imagined away.
>
> The *third* inquiry offers the answer to the question whence the ascetic ideal, the priests' ideal, derives its tremendous *power* although it is the *harmful* ideal *par excellence*, a will to the end, an ideal of decadence. Answer: not, as people may believe, because God is at work behind the priests but *faute de mieux* – because it was the only ideal so far, because it had no rival. (EH "Why I Write Such Good Books", on GM)

We shall have reason to return to consideration of the opening paragraph of this gloss shortly but for the moment let us note merely that Nietzsche here affirms that each essay is directed at a specific aspect of "morality" and at beliefs that people *may* have concerning "morality".

We can introduce some more precision into this initial characterization of the structure of the *Genealogy* by considering the target of Nietzsche's project of re-evaluation. By the time Nietzsche comes to compose this work, he identifies "morality" in terms of the following features:

(a) An identification of moral action as unegoistic, that is, in terms of "selflessness, self-denial, self-sacrifice, or sympathy and compassion" (GS §345; see also D §§79, 145–8, 215; GS §21; BGE §§33 and 55).

(b) An interpretation of suffering as punishment and, hence, the centrality of the mechanism of guilt to moral reflection (D §§29, 77–8, 89, 321; GS §135).

(c) A view of moral agency as composed of, and hence to be judged in terms of, the intentional choices of actors characterized by freedom of will (GS §127; BGE §32).

(d) The valuation of "slave" values (e.g. obedience and humility) as intrinsic values and the devaluation of "noble" values (e.g. commanding and boldness) (BGE §§195 and 260).

(e) A conception of intrinsic values as unconditioned and, hence, of moral obligations as unconditional (GS §5; BGE §§31, 46, 199, 202; GS §§344 and 347).

(f) A conception of morality as universally applicable (BGE §§198–202, 259; GS §345).

These features of "morality"[1] are all taken up in arguments in the *Genealogy*; each essay focusing on a subset of these features. The opening essay, "'Good and Evil,' 'Good and Bad'", taking as its *primum mobile* the re-evaluation of *noble* values out of the spirit of *ressentiment*, focuses on (c) and (d); the second essay, "Guilt, Bad Conscience and the Like", taking as its *primum mobile* the psychology of conscience, is directed at (a) and (b); the third essay, "What is the Meaning of Ascetic Ideals?", taking as its *primum mobile* the ascetic ideal, concerns (e) and (f). I say "broadly speaking" since issues relating to features other than those they foreground also appear in each essay and this is perhaps to be expected in so far as Nietzsche's strategy of focusing on specific aspects of "morality" in each essay means that other features that are saliently related to the aspects under

69

scrutiny will also tend to make supporting appearances (this is especially the case with the identification of morality as unegoistic, which appears in each essay). Moreover, to the extent that the three essays also comprise, albeit implicitly, a narrative concerning the formation of "morality" in which Nietzsche tracks the emergence of bad conscience (second essay), the slave revolt in morality (first essay) and the construction of the ascetic ideal (third essay) as, roughly, successive stages in the formation of "morality", this feature of his text should not surprise us.[2]

In the light of these remarks on the distinctive focus of each essay, we can return to the opening paragraph of the passage from *Ecce Homo* cited above in order to elucidate two further features of the structure of the *Genealogy* that relate to our earlier discussion of Nietzsche's elaboration of the demands of the project of re-evaluating morality. The first feature concerns Nietzsche's announcement that each essay is oriented to letting "a *new* truth" appear; an announcement that suggests – in the context of our claim that the project of re-evaluation requires that Nietzsche supply an argument that appeals to an intrinsic value within the perspective of "morality" that is also an intrinsic value within his own perspective – that it is *truthfulness* that plays this role. Nietzsche stresses this commitment on his part throughout the preface to the *Genealogy* and the centrality of this commitment to "morality" and its self-overcoming in the third essay (see GM III §27). Moreover, Nietzsche's references to his essays as opposing what people *may* believe indicate that his general strategy in the *Genealogy* depends on the commitment to truthfulness of his audience. It might be objected here that the critical function of Nietzsche's genealogy of morality requires only that his audience is committed to the intrinsic value of truth and not that Nietzsche is so committed, but such an objection runs up against both the textual evidence of the preface to, and third essay of, the *Genealogy*, in which Nietzsche makes it plain that it is this commitment to truthfulness that drives his turn to the project of re-evaluation, and the philosophical problem that unless truthfulness is an intrinsic value for Nietzsche, his project of re-evaluation will not possess the right kind of reflective stability.

The second feature to which the remarks from *Ecce Homo* draw attention can be elucidated by taking up a suggestion proposed by Chris Janaway who argues that each of the essays that compose the *Genealogy* can be read in the light of the following passage from *Beyond Good and Evil*:

> "How could anything originate out of its opposite?" ... The fundamental faith of the metaphysicians is *the faith in opposite values* ... [But] it might even be possible that what constitutes the value of these good and revered things is precisely that they are insidiously related, tied to, and involved with these wicked, seemingly opposite things – maybe even one with them in essence. Maybe!
>
> (BGE §2, cited in this form in Janaway 2003: 272)

Janaway's cogent proposal is that each of the three essays of the *Genealogy* provides a demonstration of how something "good and revered" is "tied to" precisely what it involves rejecting as "wicked, seemingly opposite things". Thus, as Janaway (2003) argues, the first essay attempts to show that the notion of the good invoked in the slave revolt is motivated in the same way as that which it rejects as evil. Similarly, as Nietzsche announces in the passage from *Ecce Homo* cited above, the voice of (bad) conscience is to be explained as a product of cruelty (Janaway 2007a). And we can extend this thought to the third essay, in which Nietzsche tries to establish that the claim to be unconditional and universal on the part of "morality", its metaphysical denial of perspective, is the product of the conditionally valuable and all-too-partial perspective of the ascetic priest.

These claims will be substantiated in the following three chapters but for our current purposes we can note that in seeking to provide accounts of this type Nietzsche is not only deploying his general strategy of appealing to the truthfulness of his audience, their will to truth, in order to undermine "morality", but also more specific strategies designed to promote a cognitive problematization of, and affective reaction against, "morality" in terms of its own constituent commitment to the "immorality" of *ressentiment*, cruelty and partiality. In this respect, and to the extent that these claims can be substantiated, Nietzsche's genealogical investigations of "morality" aim to provide accounts that perform *internal* criticisms of "morality". The form of such a criticism has been usefully elucidated by Geuss in relation to the first essay of the *Genealogy* as follows:

> [Nietzsche's] criticism is "genetic" because it appeals to a purported fact about the "origin" of Christianity – that Christianity arises from hatred, envy, resentment, and feelings of weakness and inadequacy. ... How do we know that these motives are "unacceptable"? Nietzsche, in presenting

this criticism, need not himself be committed to the view that hatred is in general, or always, or even ever an acceptable motive for beliefs, preferences and attitudes. Since it is a central doctrine of Christianity that agents ought to be motivated by love and not by hatred, resentment, envy, etc., Christianity itself gives the standard of "acceptability" for motives in the light of which it is criticized.
(Geuss 1981: 44; see also in this context Hoy 1994)

It is important to stress the point that, unlike the value of truthfulness, which must be a component of both the perspective of "morality" and Nietzsche's perspective, the view of *ressentiment*, cruelty and partiality as "immoral" need not be a judgement endorsed from Nietzsche's perspective but only from the perspective of "morality" for it to perform the critical work of bringing Nietzsche's audience to a rejection of "morality", that is, of persuading them of the need for a re-evaluation of values. Moreover, as Janaway has also stressed, this rhetorical strategy of deploying the affects cultivated by Christianity against "morality" in the rhetorical climax of each essay – "eventually a *tempo feroce* is attained in which everything rushes ahead in a tremendous tension" – expresses Nietzsche's recognition that, given that it is our inherited moral feelings that are the proximal basis of moral actions and reactions, his project of re-evaluation must engage the (existing) affects of his audience if it is to motivate their practical recognition of the need for re-evaluation (Janaway 2003; esp. 273–5 for his treatment of GM I §14).

It should perhaps be noted at this point that the view of genealogy indicated by these preliminary remarks, namely, as a mode of enquiry that integrally engages in internal criticism, is by no means uncontested. Thus, for example, Leiter (2002) defends the thesis that the *Genealogy* operates a form of external criticism that, at root, simply expresses Nietzsche's own preferred values.[3] Or, again, (later) Geuss argues that this feature of internal criticism is only incidental rather than integral to the purpose of genealogy:

To be sure, a genealogy *can* undermine various *beliefs* about the origin of different forms of valuation. If I have a certain form of valuation I may need to believe certain things – if I am a Christian I may need to believe certain things about the origin of Christian valuation. So if those beliefs are undermined, I may feel my values undermined, too, but this is as it were *my* problem, not part of the intention of genealogy. (1999a: 20)

72

I shall return to these rival views in Chapter 8. For the moment, however, having provided a sketch of the structure of the *Genealogy* and some signposts for the reading of it to be advanced in the following chapters, we can turn to the task of substantiating this view.

CHAPTER FIVE

The first essay:
"'Good and Evil', 'Good and Bad'"

The first essay, "'Good and Evil', 'Good and Bad'", focuses on the emergence of the values and conception of agency that compose the idea of the moral person invoked in "morality" through an analysis of the re-evaluation of antique values wrought by the slave revolt in morality. However, it begins with two related methodological criticisms of the "English psychologists, to whom we owe the only attempts so far to develop a history of the genesis of morality" (GM I §1).[1] Nietzsche illustrates this criticism by focusing on an argument from Rée's *The Origin of Moral Feeling* (1877), which had been endorsed by Nietzsche in *The Wanderer and his Shadow* (§40), which claimed that originally:

> "… unegoistic actions were acclaimed and described as good by those towards who they were directed, thus those to whom they were *useful*. The origin of this acclaim was later forgotten and unegoistic actions were simply felt to be good, because they were *habitually* praised as such – as if they were in themselves something good." (GM I §2)

Nietzsche's objections to this hypothesis are twofold. First, it exhibits the "*essentially* unhistorical manner" of thinking exhibited by such approaches in that it identifies the origin of morality in terms of its current value or function despite the fact that Darwin has alerted us to the point that there need be no relationship between the current function or value of a phenomenon and its original function or value (GM I §2). To this first methodological point, Nietzsche adds a second criticism, namely, that this account is psychologically unrealistic in that it is hard to see how – and why – human beings would come to forget that such "moral" actions were useful since such utility would be perpetually present to them in their "daily experience" (GM I §3). In this second respect, Nietzsche suggests that, although implausible on other grounds, Herbert Spencer's argument that we identify the concepts "good" and "useful" offers a better account by virtue of at least being psychologically plausible (*ibid*.). These criticisms indicate that Nietzsche's own investigations will function under two methodological constraints: first, a historical rule that acknowledges that the function or value of (some aspect of) "morality" at origin has no necessary relationship to its current function or value and, secondly, a psychological rule that stresses the requirement of realism in the construction of hypotheses concerning the formation of "morality".[2] The operation of these methodological rules can be seen in the structure of Nietzsche's genealogy of "morality" in that each of the three essays provide an account of the origin of a central element of "morality" in which its original function or value is distinct from the current function or value of "morality" and each essay appeals to distinct aspects of our psychological make-up in giving its account.

Recalling Nietzsche's remarks from *Ecce Homo*, we may wish, at this stage, to ask in what sense this opening of the first essay is "*calculated* to mislead". The appropriate response is that this beginning "makes it appear that we are in a scientific, objective study of the past, a sort of history or anthropology, cool and *wissenschaftlich*, as Nietzsche says", whereas "what will really be transacted is a calling into consciousness of the reader's affects" (Janaway 2003: 262),[3] which, one should add, involves enabling them to free themselves from their captivity to (since captivated by) the Christian moral perspective. To establish this point, we need to turn to Nietzsche's argument.

I

In contrast to the hypothesis advanced by the unhistorical "English psychologists", Nietzsche's hypothesis is that the judgement "good" "does *not* derive from those to whom 'goodness' is shown!"; rather:

> the "good" themselves – that is, the noble, the powerful, the superior and the high-minded – were the ones who felt themselves and their actions to be good – that is, as of the first rank – and posited them as such, in contrast to everything low, low-minded, common and plebian. (GM I §2)

It is, Nietzsche goes on to claim, "only with the decline of aristocratic value-judgments that this whole opposition between 'egoistic' and 'unegoistic' comes to impose itself on the human conscience" (GM I §2). Nietzsche credits attention to the *etymology* of concepts designating "good" to putting him on the right track, noting that it is not until, roughly, "the time of the Thirty Years War [1618–48]" that the current use of the concept "good" to denote unegoistic action becomes dominant.[4] To support this hypothesis, Nietzsche needs to provide a psychologically compelling account of the emergence of this noble mode of evaluation and of how it becomes subject to the challenge of another mode of evaluation that, eventually, issues in our current identification of the "good" and the "unegoistic".

The first step in this account hangs on the combination of a historical assumption and a psychological claim. The historical assumption is that a post-tribal political community (for Nietzsche, a state)[5] is characterized by a political hierarchy, an order of rank, which differentiates (at least) between nobles and slaves. The psychological claim is "the rule that the political concept of rank always transforms itself into a spiritual concept of rank" (GM I §6). Nietzsche's thought is that the nobles, as the highest political rank, are characterized by "the pathos of nobility and distance, the enduring, dominating, and fundamental feeling of a higher ruling kind in relation to a lower kind, to a 'below'" (GM I §2), a pathos that is unreflectively internalized as a feeling of spiritual (i.e. ethical) superiority and expressed as the valuing of what the nobility identify as their own typical character traits (GM I §5):[6] "the noble's power over others is interpreted by him as virtue, as a signification of his own goodness" (Ridley 1998a: 16). In terms of Nietzsche's doctrine of will to power, we can put this claim as follows: the nobility are characterized by the self-reflexive experience of themselves as agents and, moreover, as agents who command and utilize those of lower political rank, most obviously slaves; on the basis of this experience of themselves, the nobility identify as intrinsically valuable those traits that express their agency and understand their "spiritual" superiority in terms of their possession of these ethically valuable traits or, as they are now designated, "virtues". While the concept "good" is identified with these (newly coined) virtues and emerges "spontaneously and in advance" from the self-affirmation of the nobility, the concept "bad" simply marks an afterthought that names the absence of the character traits in question (GM I §11).

Nietzsche's account of the noble mode of valuation is not limited, however, to an account of the virtues that they coin and endorse. It is an equally central part of this account that this mode of valuation involves a specific conception of agency in which it is construed as the expression of character. In blunt terms: how one acts *is* what one is.[7] This conception of agency is not incidental to the noble mode of valuation but crucial to it in that it is this understanding of agency that articulates the translation of political superiority into spiritual superiority by supporting the identification of the political agency of the nobility with their ethical character. While Nietzsche presents this as a relatively unreflective process on the part of the nobility of antiquity, his elucidation brings it to reflective consciousness for his readers precisely in order to ensure that they can grasp the character of the counter-movement that he refers to as "the slave-revolt in morals" (GM I §10).

The re-evaluation of noble values begins, Nietzsche tells us, "when *ressentiment* becomes creative and ordains values: the *ressentiment* of creatures to whom the real reaction, that of the deed, is denied and who find compensation in an imaginary revenge" (GM I §10). We can explicate this claim in terms of the feeling of powerlessness that characterizes the slaves. First, since the slaves are subject to commands of the nobles, they do not experience their agency as intrinsically their *own*, that is, they experience themselves, for the most part, as subject to the arbitrary alien will of another. Secondly, in terms of the dominant cultural ethic (i.e. a noble morality that valorizes the typical character traits of the noble class and identifies character with agency), the capacities and dispositions that the slaves exhibit as slaves – those that typify them as a class – are seen as possessing merely instrumental, rather than intrinsic, value. More directly, the slaves experience themselves as objects of disdain. It is against this background that Nietzsche suggests that the slaves' condition is experienced by them as intolerable, generating feelings of *ressentiment*, but since these feelings of *ressentiment* cannot typically (Spartacus notwithstanding) be given outward expression, they turn inward and become creative, which is to say that they seek and find an alternative mode of expression.[8]

The creativity in question takes the form of constructing (from materials already conceptually available)[9] a perspective in which two principles of judgement combine. The first comprises a picture of the subject as characterized by voluntarism, the ability to choose freely when and how to act:

> *Bound* to do so by his instinct for self-preservation and self-affirmation, an instinct that habitually sanctifies every lie,

this kind of man discovered his faith in the indifferent, freely choosing "subject". The subject (or, to adopt a more popular idiom, the *soul*) has, therefore, been perhaps the best article of faith on earth so far, since it enables the majority of mortals, the weak and down-trodden of all sorts, to practise that sublime self-deception – the interpretation of weakness itself as freedom, of the way they simply are, as *merit*.

(GM I §13)

This picture allows the slave, on the one hand, to hold the nobles responsible for their actions on the grounds that they, the nobles, could have freely chosen not to act in this way and, on the other hand, to construe their own inability to act as the nobles act as the product of a free choice on their part. This picture, thus, allows the slaves to experience themselves as agents but also, and crucially, to evaluate the nobles as evil for choosing to act as they do and, *hence*, to evaluate themselves as good for choosing not to act in this way (GM I §11). Consequently, the slaves are able to construct a second principle of judgement comprising an evaluative picture in which it is the typical traits of the slave class that constitute the virtues and the typical traits of the noble class that are vices. Thus, on the basis of this re-evaluation, the slaves are able not only to experience themselves as agents but also to experience their agency as intrinsically valuable.

There are a number of important points to note concerning Nietzsche's analysis. The first point, oriented to warding off a common misunderstanding, is to note that Nietzsche's argument is entirely general. It is not that there is something naturally slavish about those who constitute the slave class: they are simply those who happen to have been on the wrong end of the violent constitution of the state (see GM II §17) and *anyone* placed in the position of the slave class would be compelled to engage in the kind of imaginary revenge that they accomplish as a necessary condition of making sense of themselves as agents whose agency is intrinsically valuable. The second, closely related, point is that what makes the slave revolt in morality necessary is their feeling of powerlessness and this – in the case of the slaves[10] – is a product of the non-recognition of the slaves by the nobles as agents and the non-recognition of the slaves by either the nobles or the slaves themselves within the terms of the dominant noble morality as beings who have anything but instrumental value. This failure to recognize the slaves is, moreover, *structural* in the sense that the failure to recognize the slaves as agents (rather than instruments) is a constitutive feature of the noble morality described in this essay. Indeed, Nietzsche notes that the nobles' contempt for the powerless leads them to misjudge "on occasion the sphere it despises": "it *falsifies* the image of those despised" (GM I §10). It is precisely for this reason that the slaves have no option but to contest the terms of moral recognition characteristic of this society and to do so in a way that accounts for their non-recognition by the nobles (i.e. they choose not to recognize us because they are evil). To this we may add, as a third point, that the slave revolt in morality provides a perspicuous example of how the feeling of power can be distinct from actual power. Thus, in one respect, nothing has changed: the slaves are still slaves subject to the arbitrary whim of their masters. But, in another respect, everything has changed: the slaves have constructed a general conceptual mechanism (i.e. the fiction or fantasy of the freely choosing subject) and developed a general mode of evaluation (i.e. the designation of their own typical traits as virtues) that allows them to experience a feeling of power. The fourth, and final, point to note is that while this morality presents itself in terms of an impartial view of value, it actually expresses the desire for vengeance, for power over the nobles.

II

Having laid out the basic lines of Nietzsche's argument, we can pause to focus in more depth on the distinct accounts of agency that characterize noble and slave moralities and the significance of the difference between these accounts. We can approach this topic by attending to two well-known consecutive passages from this essay. In the first passage, Nietzsche offers an allegorical skit on the situation and reasoning of the slaves:

> That lambs dislike great birds of prey does not seem strange: only it gives no grounds for reproaching these birds of prey for bearing off little lambs. And if the lambs say among themselves: "these birds of prey are evil; and whoever is least like a bird of prey, but rather its opposite, a lamb – would he not be good?" there is no reason to find fault with this institution of an ideal, except perhaps that the birds of prey might view it a little ironically and say: "*we* don't dislike them at all, these good little lambs; we even love them: nothing is more tasty than a tender lamb". (GM I §13)

In the next paragraph, Nietzsche presents a critical commentary on, and interpretation of, the reasoning disclosed in this allegory:

> To demand of strength that it should *not* express itself as strength, that it should *not* be a desire to overcome, a desire to throw down, a desire to become master, a thirst for enemies and resistances and triumphs, is just as absurd as to demand of weakness that it should express itself as strength. ... For just as the popular mind separates the lightning from its flash and takes the latter for an *action*, for the operation of a subject called lightning, so popular morality also separates strength from expression of strength, as if there were a neutral substratum behind the strong man, which was *free* to express strength or not do so. But there is no such substratum; there is no "being" behind doing, effecting, becoming; "the doer" is merely the fiction added to the deed – the deed is everything. The popular mind in fact doubles the deed; when it sees the lightning flash, it is the deed of a deed: it posits the same event first as cause and then a second time as its effect. ... [N]o wonder if the submerged, darkly glowering emotions of vengefulness and hatred exploit this belief for their own ends and in fact maintain no belief more ardently than the belief that *the strong man is free* to be weak and the bird of prey to be a lamb – for thus they gain the right to make the bird of prey *accountable* for being a bird of prey.
>
> (GM I §13) [11]

Two clusters of points are made in this passage and it is helpful to separate them.

The first cluster offers a critical diagnosis of the slave's concept of agency in terms of three related claims. The first claim is that slave morality involves a special and peculiar picture of human agency that is characterized by "a kind of double-counting" in constructing the idea of an agent-cause and an action-effect, where the agent-cause stands behind, and separate from, the contingent conditions in which one is embedded and produces action-effects in virtue of the operation of "the will", where "the mode of causation is that of command" (Williams 1995: 71; cf. BGE §19). The second claim is that "such a peculiar account must have a purpose, and that purpose is a moral one"; more specifically, the claim is that this picture emerges because it provides the conditions of articulacy for "a certain purified conception of blame" (Williams 1995: 72). Williams describes the relationship of this conception of blame to the picture of agency and willing at stake by noting how the position of a person (for example, a slave) who is (i) subject to harm, (ii) subject to the systematic failure of the other to acknowledge that harm as something for which reparation might be due to the victim and (iii) powerless to do anything about (i) or (ii):

> can give rise, in the victim or in someone else on behalf of the victim, to a very special fantasy of retrospective prevention … As victim, I have a fantasy of inserting into the agent an acknowledgement of me, to take the place of exactly the act that harmed me. I want to think that he might have acknowledged me, that he might have been prevented from harming me. But the idea cannot be that I might in some empirical way have prevented him: that idea presents only a regret that it was not actually so and, in these circumstances, a reminder of humiliation. The idea has to be, rather, that I, now, might change the agent from one who did not acknowledge me to one who did. This fantasied, magical, change does not actually involve changing anything, and it therefore has nothing to do with what, if anything, might have changed things. It requires simply the idea of the agent at the moment of the action, of the action that harmed me, and of the refusal of that action, all isolated from the network of circumstances in which his action was actually embedded. It involves precisely the picture of the will that has already been uncovered.
>
> (Williams 1995: 73)

The thought is thus that in being denied the true reaction, that of deeds, *ressentiment* becomes creative in the sense that it motivates the construction of this picture of the will and thus the conditions of articulacy required for an inchoate desire for revenge to re-emerge as a seemingly impartial idea of moral accountability. The third claim is that this is a (psychologically necessary) misunderstanding of human agency, that the idea of an agent-cause isolated from the circumstances in which one acts is a fiction, a version of the idea of the *causa sui* which Nietzsche describes as "the best self-contradiction hitherto imagined, a kind of logical rape and unnaturalness" (BGE §21).[12]

The points in the second cluster relate to the noble's conception of agency. It may seem that there is little to be gleaned here, yet I shall suggest that there are two significant pointers provided by this passage.

The first is that when Nietzsche writes "there is no such substratum; there is no 'being' behind doing, effecting, becoming; 'the doer' is merely the fiction added to the deed – the deed is everything", it is clear that he is not denying that there are agents. Rather he is denying that agency can be conceptualized independently of the embodied and embedded circumstances of agency, that is to say he is denying only that there are agents with free will in the sense specified by slave morality. This being so, what is the sense of the final element of this claim, "the deed is everything"? In adding this element to his claim, Nietzsche is directing us to his positive account of agency (which is also the idea of agency that is expressed by noble morality) which, at the very least, involves commitment to the claim that an agent's intentions (and inner life more generally) cannot be grasped independently of what he does. Thus Nietzsche is, on the one hand, denying that "the inner" (beliefs, intentions, value-commitments, etc.) is a separate domain that stands behind the agent's actions and, by issuing commands, causes them, and, on the other hand, asserting that "the inner" is only given determinate expression through "the outer", that is, that it is only in action that the agent's intentions become the determinate intentions that they are. Indeed, in arguing that strength cannot but express itself as strength, Nietzsche moves to the broader claim that one's deeds are constitutive of what one is. The second point to note is that it is the nobles' relatively unreflective commitment to such an understanding of agency that enables, and is expressed by, their identification of their own typical character traits as the virtues and their concomitant disdain for the slaves as lacking the virtues.

The salience of these remarks is not merely that Nietzsche shows that the intelligibility of slave morality and of noble morality is dependent on their articulation of distinct conceptions of moral agency but also that the account of moral agency in slave morality involves a fiction that, once recognized as such, can be seen as motivated by the desire for revenge.

II

At this stage, it is appropriate to consider an apparent puzzle concerning "the slave revolt in morality", namely, the question: who conducts it? The answer to this question may seem straightforward: the slaves. However, while the text of the first essay supports this claim in some respects, it also points in another direction, that is, to the figure of the priest.[13] Thus, Nietzsche's opening arguments in this essay involve constructing a contrast between two branches of nobility – knights and priests – and two types of political community – knightly (Rome) and priestly (Judea) (GM I §§6–8) – and assigning the initial emergence of the slave revolt in morality to the Jewish people and its development to Christianity (recall that in *Ecce Homo*, Nietzsche identifies the first essay as referring to "the birth of Christianity out of the spirit of *ressentiment*") (EH "Why I Write Such Good Books", on GM). Similarly the penultimate section of the essay deploys the terms "Rome" and "Judea" as stand-ins for noble and slave modes of evaluation (GM I §16).

How are we to reconcile these apparently conflicting signals? My suggestion is we can do this by distinguishing the historical and psychological aspects of Nietzsche's argument. On the one hand, Nietzsche's historical focus is directed to the history of European morality and, hence, to the issue of where and when the slave mode of valuation emerges and develops such that it becomes the dominant mode of evaluation; indeed (and I shall return to this point) such that the slave revolt in morality "has today dropped out of sight only because it – has succeeded ..." (GM I §7). In this respect, it is unsurprising that Nietzsche refers to Judaism and Christianity as the historical sources of this mode of evaluation in Europe or, indeed, that he takes Rome as the counterpoint since it is the gradual process of the succumbing of Rome to Christianity ("consider before whom one bows today in Rome as before the epitome of all the highest values", as Nietzsche remarks; GM I §16) that marks the conditions of triumph of this mode of evaluation. On the other hand, Nietzsche's psychological focus is on how this mode of evaluation emerges and why it is endorsed. Here it is his account of how the slave revolt transmutes a feeling of powerlessness into a feeling of power that does the work. While Nietzsche does take the emergence of this mode of evaluation to be historically situated (from the point of view of the history of European morality) in the context of the Jewish people, under conditions of powerlessness,[14] and in the development of (Pauline) Christianity from this priestly soil, his psychological claim is that a mode of evaluation of this type will emerge (or, if already available as, say, a foreign import, will be endorsed) from the experience of feeling powerless and subject to the disdain of the powerful.[15] Thus, from a psychological point of view, even if it is historically the case that the priest – or a priestly people – initiates the slave revolt in morality (see GS §353), Nietzsche's primary concern is to point out that the genesis (and popular appeal) of this mode of evaluation is intrinsically related to the experience of being subject to domination and to the disdain of those who dominate. In this regard, whether the slave revolt in morality is, as a matter of contingent historical fact, an autonomous product of the slave class or an interpretation of the daily existence of the slave class by a priest that is subsequently endorsed by the slave class is not a matter of significance for Nietzsche's argument in this essay.[16]

IV

Let us now, finally, turn to the claim that the opening of this essay is calculated to mislead in virtue of the fact that its apparently cool scientific character disguises that Nietzsche's aim is to engage the affects of his audience. Recall that Nietzsche takes his audience to be held captive by a particular metaphysical picture of morality that "stubbornly and ruthlessly declares 'I am morality itself and nothing else is moral!'" (BGE §202). As we have noted, all three essays of the *Genealogy* may be taken as concerned to dislodge this metaphysical picture (and we shall see in our discussion of the third essay how "morality" comes to be characterized by this stubborn and ruthless declaration); however, the more immediate issue posed by this condition of captivation is that if Nietzsche is (eventually) to bring his readers to take "morality" as an object of critical reflection and assessment, a necessary first step in this process is to demonstrate that "morality" is not the *only* form of ethical reflection and, further, to engage his readers' affects with the form of ethical reflection that he contrasts to "morality" so as to loosen and account (in part) for their captivation by this moral perspective. The demonstrative aspect of this task is accomplished by Nietzsche's account of the necessary relationship of "morality" as slave morality to noble morality, of "morality" as a counter-movement to a pre-existing form of ethical reflection and valuation. In giving this demonstration Nietzsche also accounts for one source of his readers' captivation by the perspective of "morality" – the fact that the slave revolt in morality has become invisible – by suggesting that this is itself a product of the triumph of slave morality (GM I §7). But, on Nietzsche's view, this demonstration can only do the work of loosening the grip of "morality" if it engages his readers at an affective, and not merely cognitive level. It is for this reason that the essay has a complex rhetorical composition that reaches its climax in §14.

Nietzsche's efforts to probe and guide his readers' affective responses is conducted by way of both a series of rhetorical contrasts and two staged engagements with imagined interlocutors. With respect to the former, we can note that Nietzsche characterizes the nobles in terms of self-affirmation (GM I §2), a "powerful physicality" (GM I §7), a disposition to honesty and naivety in their relationships to self and others (GM I §10), an ability to discharge or shrug off *ressentiment* (*ibid.*), a mode of conduct towards other nobles "strictly restrained by custom, respect, usage, gratitude, even more by circumspection and jealousy" and characterized by "consideration, self-control, tenderness, fidelity, pride and friendship" (GM I §11) and a mode of conduct towards strangers characterized by:

> *regress* to the innocence of the predator's conscience, as rejoicing monsters, capable of high spirits as they walk away without qualm from a horrific succession of murder, arson, violence and torture, as if it were nothing more than a student prank, something new for the poets to sing and celebrate for some time to come. (*Ibid.*)

In contrast, Nietzsche characterizes "the man of *ressentiment*" in terms of a negation of the other (GM I §§10–11), intelligence and ingenuity (GM I §7), a disposition to falsify and calculate in their relationships to self and others ("the man of *ressentiment* is neither upright nor naïve in his dealings with others, nor is he honest and open with himself. His soul *squints*; ..." ; GM I §10) and an inability to discharge or shrug off *ressentiment* (GM I §§10–11; cf. Owen 1998). What is most notable about these rhetorical contrasts that Nietzsche deploys is that he does not simply valorize noble morality by contrast to slave morality; thus, for example, he acknowledges with respect to the nobles that "[we] would be the last to deny that anyone who met these 'good men' only as enemies would know them only as *evil enemies*" and notes that the last (and perhaps greatest) exemplar of this noble morality – Napoleon – is "the incarnation of the problem of the *noble ideal as such* – consider *what* a problem it is, Napoleon, this synthesis of the *overhuman* and the *inhuman* ..." (GM I §16). Similarly, while Nietzsche is concerned to emphasize the mendacity of slave morality and its domestication of man, he also acknowledges that "[h]uman history would be a much too stupid affair were it not for the intelligence introduced by the powerless" (GM I §7). Nietzsche's strategy is, thus, to elicit both admiration for, and horror at, the nobles, and to elicit disgust at, and sympathy for, the men of *ressentiment*: disgust at their self-deception but also sympathy and even admiration for the intelligence that they bring to coping with the intolerable position that they occupy. We might note that in this respect Nietzsche displays something of the attitude towards the powerless that he attributes to the nobles:

> One should not fail to notice the almost benevolent *nuances* present in all the words with which the Greek nobility distinguishes the lower people from itself; how a kind of pity, consideration and forbearance continually intervenes and sweetens, until ultimately almost all the words applied to the common man survive as expressions meaning "unhappy", "pitiable" ... – and how, too, "bad", "low", "unhappy" have never since ceased to ring in a *single* note to the Greek ear, with a tonality in which "unhappy" predominates. This is a legacy from the old, more noble, aristocratic mode of evaluation, which refuses to deny itself even in its contempt for others .... (GM I §10)

If we turn from the rhetorical contrasts that Nietzsche deploys to the two engagements with an interlocutor that he constructs, we can see a similar pattern with respect to slave morality. The first of these imagined interlocutors intervenes in §9, following Nietzsche's initial description of Christianity as the highest expression of the "transvaluation of all values" that "has so far continued to triumph over all other ideals, over all noble ideals" (GM I §8). This "free spirit" and "democrat" endorses the view that the slave revolt in morality has succeeded and welcomes this fact; indeed, this figure bears a close relationship to the urbane atheists to whom the madman announces the death of God in Nietzsche's dramatization of this event in *The Gay Science*, in that this free spirit rejects the Church while endorsing "morality". With this passage, Nietzsche anticipates and expresses what he takes to be the likely stance – and impatient response – of his audience but redescribes "morality" in the mouth of this interlocutor in terms that link it to the Church as "its poison", suggests to the reader that "on this matter, there is much to keep silent about" (GM I §9) and proceeds in the following section to give his account of the birth of slave morality from *ressentiment*.

The second engagement with an interlocutor – Mr Daredevil Curiousity – takes the form of a dialogue in which Nietzsche:

> affects to send this member of the public down into a fetid, cavernous workshop, reminiscent of Wagner's Nibelheim,

where morality is cobbled together by shadowy, stunted creatures brimming with *ressentiment*. The authorial voice receives reports from the front-line emissary as if from the safety of surface daylight, goading him on until what he witnesses becomes unbearable and he demands to be returned to the open air.   (Janaway 2003: 273)

What Mr Daredevil Curiousity witnesses is:

the affective states of the fabricators of the ideal of the good – their fear, hate, misery, [desire for] revenge, hope, comfort – and his own affective reaction is shown through the sustained metaphor of smell, stink, "Bad air!": he is disgusted. But what disgusts him most are the lies involved in fabricating the ideal of the good. The desires that are born out of the affective states of the oppressed are for revenge, justice, judgment, kingdom – in short, power over those that oppress them.   (*Ibid.*: 274–5)

Nietzsche supports the claims of this section in the following section by citing Thomas Aquinas "'*Beati in regno coelesti videbunt poenas damnatorum, ut beatitudo illis magis complaceat*' [The blessed in the kingdom of heaven will see the punishment of the damned so they may enjoy their bliss all the more.]" (GM I §15) and Tertullian, at much greater length, to similar effect. We should be careful to note, however, that the dialogue of §14 does *not* imply that the oppressed know that they are lying or that the ideal of good is fabricated from lies; on the contrary, it is Mr Daredevil Curioisity – that is, Nietzsche's representative of us, his readers – who discerns "that lies are being told ... Weakness is to be transformed into a *merit* through lies, there is no doubt – it is just as you said" (GM I §14).[17] In this rhetorical climax to the essay, it is thus the reader who, having followed Nietzsche's account, is placed in the position of acknowledging, through the representative figure of Mr Daredevil Curiousity, the mendacity of slave morality in a way that was not possible for the slaves. To the extent that Nietzsche has provided a psychologically realistic account of the historical emergence of the aspects of "morality" – its valuation of values and its concept of moral agency – treated in this essay, the reader is brought to a condition of disgust with slave morality predicated on recognizing that these aspects of "morality" emerge from the spirit of *ressentiment* and, hence, that the claim to impartiality embodied in "morality" is mendacious.

In the penultimate section of this first essay, Nietzsche writes:

> For thousands of years, a fearful struggle has raged on earth between the two opposed value-judgments, "good and bad" and "good and evil"; and as certain as it is that the second value-judgment has been in the ascendant, there is even now no shortage of places that the conflict remains undecided. It might even be said that the conflict has escalated in the interim and so becomes increasingly profound, more spiritual: so that today there is perhaps no more decisive mark of the "*higher nature*", of the more spiritual nature, than to be divided against oneself in this sense and to remain a battleground for these oppositions. (GM I §16)

It is to this position of being "a battleground for these oppositions" that Nietzsche's rhetorical strategy has sought to move his readers: disgusted by the mendacity of slave morality yet sympathetic to its causes while admiring of its ingenuity and, at once, awestruck and horrified by the ancient form of noble morality. In seeking to dislodge his audience's captivation by "morality" without simply advocating an (impossible) return to the ancient form of noble morality, Nietzsche attempts to elicit a complex affective response from his audience in which the recognition that slave morality, like noble morality, is an expression of will to power is combined with being "divided against oneself" and, hence, open to the claim that Nietzsche advances of the need for a re-evaluation of our values.

CHAPTER SIX

The second essay: "'Guilt', 'Bad Conscience' and Related Matters"

In the second essay, "'Guilt', 'Bad Conscience' and Related Matters", Nietzsche turns from the valuations and idea of moral agency characteristic of "morality" to consider "the psychology of *conscience*" (EH "Why I Write Such Good Books", on GM). From *Daybreak* on, Nietzsche had noted that two central features of "morality" are its central reliance on guilt as an emotion of self-assessment and, indeed, its "moralization" of guilt, that is, its treatment of all forms of human suffering as necessarily explicable in terms of the legitimate punishment of guilty agents, on the one hand, and the identification of "morality" with unegoistic motivations, on the other hand. In this essay, Nietzsche will seek to provide a naturalistic explanation of "bad conscience" that accounts for these features of "morality" as products of an instinct for cruelty.

I

The essay begins with Nietzsche considering the conditions under which human beings become capable of making and holding to promises (read commitments). His starting-point is to note that the ability to make commitments presupposes a variety of capacities:

> To think in terms of causality, to see and anticipate from afar, to posit ends and means with certainty, to be able above all to reckon and calculate! For that to be the case, how much man himself must have become *calculable*, *regular*, *necessary*, even to his own mind, so that finally he would be able to vouch for

himself *as future*, in the way that someone making a promise
does! (GM II §1)

Thus the question becomes that of how the task of "*making* man to
a certain extent necessary, uniform, an equal among equals, regular
and consequently calculable" (GM II §2) is accomplished? Nietzsche's
hypothesis is that this is achieved in the prehistory of humanity "by
means of the morality of custom and the social strait-jacket" (*ibid.*). By
this, Nietzsche means simply that it was through the morality of custom
and the social straitjacket that human beings became creatures about
whom one could legitimately have normative expectations concerning
their activity since they have acquired the capacity not only for second-
order desires but also for second-order volitions. When Nietzsche
speaks of the development of "a real *memory of the will*" as:

> an ongoing willing of what was once willed ... so that between
> the original "I will", "I shall do", and the actual realization of
> the will, its *enactment*, a world of new and strange things, cir-
> cumstances, even other acts of will may safely intervene, with
> causing this long chain of will to break ... (GM II §1)

he is stressing the centrality of second-order volitions to personhood.
At the end of this process:

> where society and its morality of custom finally reveal the
> *end* to which they were merely a means: there we find as the
> ripest fruit on their tree the *sovereign individual*, the individ-
> ual who resembles no one but himself, who has once again
> broken away from the morality of custom, the autonomous
> supra-moral individual (since "autonomous" and "moral" are
> mutually exclusive) – in short, the man with his own inde-
> pendent, enduring will, whose *prerogative it is to promise*.
> (GM II §2)[1]

We shall return to the *sovereign individual* shortly. However, the
prior issue is this: how do the morality of custom and the social
straitjacket make man calculable in the relevant sense? In *Daybreak*,
Nietzsche suggested that "barbarous peoples" were characterized by
"a species of customs whose purpose appears to be custom in general:
minute and fundamentally superfluous stipulations", which "keep
continually in the consciousness the constant proximity of custom, the

perpetual compulsion to practice customs" and, hence, "strengthen the mighty proposition with which civilization begins: any custom is better than no custom" (D §16). In the *Genealogy*, the emphasis shifts to the role of punishment for breaches of custom:

> The worse mankind's memory was, the more frightening its customs appear; the harshness of punishment codes, in particular, gives a measure of how much effort it required to triumph over forgetfulness and to make these ephemeral slaves of emotion and desire mindful of a few primitive requirements of social cohabitation. (GM II §3)

Noting the spectacular economy of punishment that characterizes ancient German history (stoning, breaking on a wheel, impalement on a stake, quartering, boiling in oil, flaying, etc.), Nietzsche comments:

> With the help of such images and procedures one eventually memorizes five or six "I will not's," thus giving one's *promise* in return for the advantages offered by society. And indeed! with the help of this sort of memory, one eventually did come to "see reason"! – Ah, reason, seriousness, mastery over the emotions, the whole murky affair which goes by the name of thought, all these privileges and showpieces of man: what a high price has been paid for them! how much blood and horror is at the bottom of all "good things". (*Ibid.*)

There are two aspects to this spectacular economy of punishment worthy of note. The first is that it is a *"technique for remembering things"*, which expresses "a central proposition of the oldest (and unfortunately also the most enduring) psychology on earth", namely, "only that which *hurts* incessantly is remembered" (*ibid.*). The second concerns the relationship between this economy of punishment and coming "to 'see reason'!" This second aspect requires careful consideration since it introduces two crucial features of Nietzsche's account. Nietzsche's suggestion is that punishment in early human societies is based on a logic of equivalence between damage and pain that (i) emerges in the basic creditor–debtor relationships that constitute the first elements of a legal system and (ii) expresses the basic human instinct for cruelty.

Creditor–debtor relationships, Nietzsche hypothesizes, are the site:

where *promises* are made; at issue here is the *making* of a memory for the man who promises ... In order to instill trust for his promise of repayment, in order to give a guarantee for the seriousness and sacredness of his promise, in order to impress repayment as a duty and obligation sharply upon his own conscience, the debtor contractually pledges to the creditor in the event of non-payment something which he otherwise still "possesses", something over which he still has power – for example, his body or his wife or his freedom or even his life ... In particular, however, the creditor could subject the body of the debtor to all sorts of humiliation and torture – he could, for example, excise as much flesh as seemed commensurate with the size of the debt.   (GM II §5)

This "earliest and most primordial relationship between men" is central not only to the formation of a real memory of the will but to the formation of our ability to reason:

No civilization, however rudimentary, has been found where something of this relationship cannot be discerned. Setting prices, estimating values, devising equivalents, making exchanges – this has preoccupied the very earliest thinking of man to such an extent that it, in a certain sense, constitutes *thinking as such*: ... It was from this most rudimentary form of personal law that the budding sense of exchange, contract, debt, law, obligation, compensation first *translated* itself into the crudest and earliest social complexes (in their relation to similar complexes), along with the habit of comparing, measuring, and calculating power in relation to power. The eye was now adjusted to this perspective: and with that clumsy consistency which is peculiar to the thinking of mankind in earlier times, a thinking which is slow to get under way, but which once in motion continues relentlessly in the same direction, one soon arrives at the great generalization: "Everything has its price; *everything* can be paid off " – the earliest and most naïve canon of moral *justice*, the beginning of all "neighbourliness", all "fairness", all "good will", all "objectivity" on earth.   (GM II §8)

Nietzsche's strategy is, thus, to begin with this legal context and the kind of psychology that it involves as a way of accounting for the emergence of the ethical psychology of socialized individuals (including both the sovereign individual and, as we shall see, the man of bad conscience).

This basic creditor–debtor schema is generalized, Nietzsche suggests, over two other forms of relationship. First, the relationship of the community (creditor) to its members (debtors):

> One lives in a community ..., one lives protected, looked after, in peace and trust, without a care for certain forms of harm and hostility to which the man *outside*, the "outlaw" is exposed ... since man has pledged and committed himself to the community as regards this harm and hostility. What will happen *if the pledge is broken*? The community, the deceived creditor, will see that it receives payment, in so far as it can, one may count on that. ... The criminal is a debtor who not only fails to repay the advantages and advances offered to him but even attacks his creditors, and for that reason he is from that point not only, as is just, denied all these goods and advantages – he is also reminded of *what these goods represent*. The fury of the aggrieved creditor, of the community, returns him to the wild outlaw state from which he was previously protected: it expels him – and now every kind of hostility may be vented on him.　　　　　(GM II §9)

Secondly, the relationship of the ancestor-founders of society (creditors) to its current members (debtors):

> Here the conviction prevails that the race only *exists* by virtue of the sacrifice and achievements of the forefathers – and that one is obliged to *repay* them through sacrifice and achievements: a *debt* is recognized, which gnaws incessantly by virtue of the fact that these forefathers, in their continued existence as powerful spirits, never cease to grant the race new advantages and advances in strength. ... According to this kind of logic, the *fear* of the forefather and of his power, the consciousness of indebtedness towards him necessarily increases, as the race itself becomes ever-more victorious, independent, respected, feared ... – ultimately, the forefather is necessarily transfigured into a *god*.　　　　　(GM II §19)

Notice that both of these analogical applications of the creditor–debtor relationship exhibit the logic of equivalence manifest in the legal creditor–debtor relationship, in which the failure to repay fully one's debt *entitles* the creditor to inflict pain on the debtor. What grounds this logic of equivalence, Nietzsche argues, is that pleasure that the creditor derives from "the opportunity to *inflict* suffering" (GM II §6) on the debtor, where this pleasure is the feeling of power that attends giving expression to the instinct for cruelty: "the pleasure of being able to vent his power without a second thought on one who is powerless" (GM II §5). If the creditor is not himself a member of the nobility, this pleasure "will be prized all the more highly" since by means "of the 'punishment' inflicted on a debtor, the creditor partakes of a *privilege of the masters*: at last, he too has the opportunity to experience the uplifting feeling of being entitled to despise and mistreat someone as 'beneath him'" (*ibid.*; cf. also GM II §6). Thus, "the compensation consists in an entitlement and right to cruelty" (GM II §5).

On Nietzsche's account, then, it is through a social context characterized by the legal, political and religious forms of the creditor–debtor relationship, and the systems of punishment that characterize these relationships, that human beings develop a memory of the will and the capacity to reason as well as a standard of value predicated on the entitlement to make commitments. The emergence of conscience, that is, "the capacity to make oneself the object of one's own consciousness and a corresponding potential to make oneself the object of one's own will" (Ridley 1998a: 15), is provided here with a basis in the naturalistic hypothesis of will to power in conjunction with some plausible conjectures concerning early human societies.

II

At this stage, let us return to the figure of the *sovereign individual*, whom Nietzsche presents as the ripe, late, fruit of this process. This figure represents the concept of the autonomous individual who is not bound by moral rules as customary constraints but as the freely endorsed commitments through which he gives expression to his own character. The *sovereign individual* exhibits "a proud consciousness, tense in every muscle, of *what* has been finally achieved here, of what has become incarnate in him – a special consciousness of power and freedom, a feeling of the ultimate completion of man" (GM II §2). Nietzsche continues:

> This liberated man who has the *prerogative* to promise, this master of *free* will, this sovereign – how should he not be aware of his superiority over everything which cannot promise and vouch for itself? How should he not be aware of how much trust, how much fear, how much respect he arouses – he *"deserves"* all three – and how much mastery over circumstances, over nature, and over all less reliable creatures with less enduring wills is necessarily given into his hands along with this self-mastery. (*Ibid.*)

Given this consciousness, Nietzsche concludes this passage by drawing attention to the criteria of evaluation of persons deployed by the sovereign individual:

> The "free" man – the owner of an enduring indestructible will – possesses also in the property his *measure of value*: looking out at others from his own vantage point, he bestows respect or contempt. Necessarily, he respects those who are like himself – the strong and reliable (those with the *prerogative* to promise), that is, anyone who promises like a sovereign ... who is sparing with his trust, who *confers distinction* when he trusts, who gives his word as something which can be relied on, because he knows himself strong enough to uphold it even against accidents, even "against fate". Even so, he will keep the toe of his boot poised for the cowering dogs who make promises without entitlement, and hold his stick at the ready for the liar who breaks his word the moment he utters it. The proud knowledge of this extraordinary privilege of *responsibility*, the consciousness of this rare freedom, this power over oneself and over fate has sunk down into his innermost depths and has become an instinct, a dominant instinct – what will he call it, this dominant instinct, assuming he needs a name for it? About that there can be no doubt: this sovereign man calls it his *conscience* ... (*Ibid.*)

In one respect, the evaluative contrast drawn in Nietzsche's discussion of the sovereign individual is between those who are entitled to *represent* themselves "to others as holding certain beliefs or attitudes" or commitments and those who "do not have the same right to speak in this way on their own behalf" (Lovibond 2002: 71). As Sabina Lovibond puts it:

Only on condition that I have, for example, sufficient self-control (or courage or energy) to carry out some declared intention of mine can I credibly give myself out as *someone who is going to act that way* ("Don't worry, I won't get into an argument about ..."); if the condition is not met, others will do better to disregard my words in favour of whatever locally relevant knowledge they may have of my involvement in the "realm of law" (say, the number of drinks, hours or minutes of dinner party, or whatever that it usually takes to crack my thin veneer of cool). (*Ibid.*: 72)[2]

The sovereign individual, as the positive pole of Nietzsche's contrast, refers to "the condition of 'self-mastery' or full competence to represent oneself to the rest of the world" (*ibid.*: 74).[3] At the negative pole of Nietzsche's contrast, it seems, stands "the liar who breaks his word the moment he utters it" (GM II §2), that is, in contemporary philosophical parlance: the wanton (Frankfurt 1988: 11–25). There is, I think, little doubt that Nietzsche draws this contrast in such extreme terms in order to heighten our attraction to the figure of the sovereign individual and our repulsion from the figure of the wanton, but in doing so he raises a puzzle to which Ridley (2007b) has drawn attention, namely, what is distinctive about the sovereign individual's promise-making? Since it is the case that the vast majority of socialized individuals are not wantons, that is, are capable of making and, *ceteris paribus*, keeping promises, and since Nietzsche, as we have seen, spends some time in this essay explaining how this comes to be the case, what is it that distinguishes the sovereign individual?

In the first essay of the *Genealogy* (and elsewhere), Nietzsche ascribes to noble morality, and himself endorses, an account of agency in which one's deeds are seen as criterial of one's intentions, beliefs, desires and so on (see Pippin 2004). On this view, as Ridley points out, "if it is essential to a promise's being made in good faith that the agent intend to act on it, it is essential, too, that – *ceteris paribus* – he does indeed so act" (Ridley 2007b: 4). If, however, the figure of the sovereign individual represents a self-conscious condition of self-mastery, this entails a specific kind of understanding of the *ceteris paribus* clause, that is, one in which the range of excuses to which one can have recourse is limited to reasons that are compatible with the presumption of self-mastery. There are thus two main types of excuse that could justify the failure to maintain a commitment, which relate to conditions of causal and normative necessity, respectively.

The first is that honouring one's commitment is causally impossible due to circumstances beyond one's control; hence, one cannot *physically* do what is required (say, fly from London to New York today to be best man at a wedding since all flights are cancelled due to a terrorist attack). The second is that keeping one's promises is normatively impossible due to circumstances beyond one's control; hence, one must not *ethically* do what is required (say, ignore the drowning child in order to fulfil the obligation to meet a friend for a quiet drink and chat). Notice that a further implication of this self-understanding is that, even in circumstances where the reasons for breach of one's commitment are exculpatory, the sovereign individual acknowledges a debt to the addressee of their commitment and, thus, an acknowledgment that reparations may be due. This claim is supported by Nietzsche's characterization of the sovereign individual as:

> anyone who promises like a sovereign ... who is sparing with his trust, who *confers distinction* when he trusts, who gives his word as something which can be relied on, because he knows himself strong enough to uphold it even against accidents, even "against fate".   (GM II §2)

The point here is not *per impossible* that the sovereign individual has (or is committed to) mastery over fate in general – a fantasy of which Nietzsche would be entirely dismissive – but that the sovereign individual is characterized by a degree of prudence in their commitment-making activity (that is, a serious effort to consider, as far as possible, the types of circumstance in which the commitment is to be honoured and the range of costs that may arise in fulfilment of the commitment as well as its prospects for conflicting with existing commitments), where this prudence is engendered precisely by an acknowledgment of one's responsibility as extending to those occasions on which the commitment cannot or must not be honoured. Upholding one's word "even 'against fate'" does not mean fantastically committing oneself to the incoherent goal of doing what is causally or ethically impossible for one to do; it means willingly bearing responsibility for the damage incurred when one's commitment cannot or must not be kept. This is a stance that acknowledges and affirms the fatality of one's agency rather than seeking to avoid or deny it.

In relation to this first aspect of the distinctiveness of the sovereign individual, Nietzsche's position may be aligned with a point that Williams pressed against "the morality system" whose standpoint he describes as granting no special significance to the thought *I did it* and hence, as turning "our attention away from an important dimension of ethical experience, which lies in the distinction between what one has and what one has not done", a distinction that "can be as important as the distinction between the voluntary and the non-voluntary" (Williams 1985: 177). Williams illustrates this point with the example of Ajax, following his goddess-deranged slaughter of a flock of sheep:

> Ajax then wakes up and shows that he has recovered his mind. There is a passionate lyric outburst of despair and, above all, shame: he has made himself, apart from anything else, utterly absurd. It becomes increasingly clear to himself that he can only kill himself. He knows that he cannot change his *ethos*, his character, and he knows that after what he has done, this grotesque humiliation, he cannot lead the only kind of life his *ethos* demands. ... Being what he is, he could not live as a man who had done these things; it would be merely impossible, in virtue of the relations between what he expects of the world and what the world expects of a man who expects that of it. (Williams 1993: 72–3)

Williams's point is not that we should endorse Ajax's suicide but that we should acknowledge the ethical intelligibility of Ajax's response and, hence, the weight that *I did it* can play in our ethical lives. For our immediate concerns, the point is this: the sovereign individual is one for whom the thought *I did it* has ethical purchase and salience.

There is, however, another dimension of the sovereign individual's promise-making that deserves attention and that hangs on the expressive account of agency to which Nietzsche is committed. This dimension can be drawn out by contrasting promises whose accomplishment conditions (i.e. the conditions that entitle one to say that the promise has been kept) can and cannot be specified externally (i.e. in advance and independently of the execution of the accomplishment). If I promise to meet you today for lunch in the pub, the accomplishment conditions can be specified externally: I have kept my promise if I turn up at the pub in order to eat with you within the relevant time frame. In contrast, if I promise to love and honour you until death us do part, then what counts as keeping this promise cannot be fully specified in advance and independently of a particular way of keeping it. In the former case, keeping my promise simply confirms the presence of my intention; in the latter case, *the nature of my intention is revealed in the way that I keep it*. What is distinctive about the sovereign individual in this respect is that his most characteristic form of promise-making is of the latter type; indeed, it is precisely the sovereign individual's self-mastery that entitles him to engage in this kind of promise-making (Ridley 2007b: 6–10). Notice, though, that another way of drawing the distinction between the two kinds of promise-making invoked here is to specify them in terms of commitments whose character is fully determined by the letter of the law and commitments whose character can only be fully determined by reference to both the letter and spirit of the law (*ibid.*: 10). As Ridley comments, using the example of marriage:

> It is true that there are some independently specifiable success-conditions here (although they are defeasible). Respect is presumably necessary, for example, as are caring for the other person's interest and not betraying them, say. But what exactly might *count* as betrayal, or what caring for the other person's interests might *look* like in this case – or even whether *these* things are what is at issue – cannot be specified independently of the particular marriage that it is, of the circumstances, history and personalities peculiar to it, and of how those things unfold or develop over time. It is, in other words, perfectly possible that everything I do is, as it were, strictly speaking respectful, considerate and loyal, and yet that I fail to be any good as a husband – I am true to the letter but miss the spirit, as we might say. (*Ibid.*)

This helps to draw out the sense in which the sovereign individual can be represented by Nietzsche as the ethical *telos* of the process of socialization that he is exploring in this essay, since the freedom enjoyed and exemplified by the sovereign individual is only available to persons who are, in Ridley's phrase, "socialized … all the way down", that is, have internalized the norms constitutive of the social practices and institutions in and through which they act (in this case, that of marriage). In sum, then, the sovereign individual's entitlement to make promises consists "in his capacity to commit himself whole-heartedly to undertakings whose character is inconceivable except in the context of the institutions from which they draw their sense" (*ibid.*: 11).[4]

This second dimension of distinctiveness enables us to see once again that Nietzsche is articulating a view of ethical autonomy that contrasts sharply with the ideal of moral autonomy expressed in Kant, and which Nietzsche takes to be representative of "morality". This is so because it directs attention to the fact that the central role of the categorical imperative in Kantian morality entails that if:

> I find that the maxim of my action cannot be universalized without contradiction, I have identified an absolute prohibition, an unconditional "I will not". I have, in other words, stopped short at a formulable instruction that might be fully obeyed by anyone ... The spirit ... has gone missing without trace. (*Ibid.*: 12)

We can put the point like this: "morality" in the sense exemplified by Kant may have liberated itself from the morality of custom as regards to *content* but it has not done so with regard to *form*. Moral freedom for Kant, Nietzsche charges, can be articulated in terms of compliance with a list of "I will not's" that can be specified in advance and independently of the way in which commitment to them is executed. In this respect, Kant's philosophy exhibits the characteristic errors of "morality", namely, a failure to acknowledge the expressive character of human agency combined with a stress on the unconditional character of moral imperatives, and does so in a way that leaves it blind to the nature and experience of human freedom as an unformulable process of self-legislation.

The initial impetus towards the rejection of an expressive account of human agency has been accounted for in the first essay, and in the third essay Nietzsche will focus on the attractions of the view of moral imperatives as universal and unconditional. However, in the remainder of the second essay, Nietzsche focuses on the related topic of the emergence of *bad conscience* and it is to this that we now, finally, turn. Before doing so, though, we can once again ask ourselves in what sense the beginning of Nietzsche's essay, this rhetorical move of starting with the figure of the sovereign individual, is intended to mislead. In contrast to the first essay, Nietzsche does not mean here to lead us to think mistakenly that we are being given a certain kind of cool and impersonally objective history; rather, Nietzsche misleads us in the sense of sketching an ideal to which we will be attracted and in which we would like to see ourselves before pulling the rug from beneath our feet and presenting to us a painfully contrasting image of ourselves in the figure of the man of *bad conscience*.

III

Nietzsche's initial hypothesis concerning *bad conscience* is that it is "the deep sickness to which man was obliged to succumb under the pressure of the most fundamental of all changes – when he found himself definitively locked in the spell of society and peace" (GM II §16). Such enclosure entails, Nietzsche hypothesizes, that the instincts of these "half-animals who were happily adapted to a life of wilderness, war, nomadism and adventure" in virtue of being unable to express themselves, turn inwards:

> Every instinct which does not vent itself externally *turns inwards* – this is what I call the *internalization* of man: it is at this point that what is latter called the "soul" first develops in man. The whole inner world, originally stretched thinly as between two membranes, has extended and expanded, has acquired depth, breadth, and height in proportion as the external venting of human instinct has been *inhibited*. Those fearful bulwarks by means of which the state organization protected itself against the old instincts of freedom – punishment belongs above all to these bulwarks – caused all the instincts of the wild, free, nomadic man to turn backwards *against man himself*. Hostility, cruelty, pleasure in persecution, in assault, in change, in destruction – all that turning against the man who possesses such instincts: *such* is the origin of "bad conscience".   (*Ibid.*)

How is this change, this sudden change, wrought? Nietzsche's hypothesis is that it is the product of a violent process of state-formation in which:

> some horde or other of blond predatory animals, a race of conquerors and masters which, itself organized for war and with the strength to organize others, unhesitatingly lays its fearful claws on a population that may be hugely superior in numerical terms but remains shapeless and nomadic.   (GM II §17)

As Nietzsche goes on to insist:

> [The horde] were not the ones among whom "bad conscience" grew up, as goes without saying from the outset – but it would not have grown up *without them*, this ugly weed, it would not

exist if, under the force of their hammer blows, of their artists' violence, a vast quantity of freedom had not been expelled from the world, or at least removed from visibility and, as it were, forcibly made *latent*. This *instinct for freedom* made latent through force – as we have already understood – this instinct for freedom, forced back, trodden down, incarcerated within and ultimately still venting and discharging itself only upon itself: such is *bad conscience* at its origin, that and nothing more.   (*Ibid.*)

Now, at this point in his argument, it may seem that Nietzsche has boxed himself into something of a corner. After all, referring to these conquerors as "the most involuntary, most unconscious artists there are" (*ibid.*) does not deflect the point that the activity of forming the shapeless mass of nomads that they have conquered into the subjects of a state by, for example, imposing customs on them, entails that these conquerors themselves are able to make promises (that is what imposing a custom involves) and, hence, must be characterized by that degree of internalization that the formation of conscience (i.e. being subject to "the morality of custom and the social straight-jacket") involves.

There is, however, a crucial distinction between these conquering nobles and the man of *ressentiment*, to whom Nietzsche attributes the development of bad conscience, and Nietzsche has already supplied two indications of this difference. In the second essay itself, as we have noted, Nietzsche refers to the non-noble creditor as one who "partakes of a *privilege of the masters*: at last, he too has the opportunity to experience the uplifting feeling of being entitled to despise and mistreat someone as 'beneath him'" (GM II §5; cf. also GM II §6). The implication is that the nobles are able to express the human instinct for cruelty within society, at least on their slaves. However, the most important statement of this difference came in the first essay where Nietzsche comments:

We would be the last to deny that anyone who met these "good men" only as enemies would know them only as *evil enemies*, and that these same men, who are *inter pares* so strictly restrained by custom, respect, usage, gratitude, even more by circumspection and jealously, and who in their relations with one another prove so inventive in matters of consideration, self-control, tenderness, fidelity, pride, and friendship – these same men behave towards the outside world – where the foreign, the *foreigners*, are to be found – in a manner not much better than predators on the rampage. There they enjoy freedom from all social constraint, in the wilderness they make up for the tension built up over a long period of confinement and enclosure within a peaceful community, they *regress* to the innocence of the predator's conscience, as rejoicing monsters, capable of high spirits as they walk away without qualms from a horrific succession of murder, arson, violence, and torture, as if it were nothing more than a student prank, something new for the poets to sing and celebrate for some time to come.

(GM I §11)

The distinction is, thus, between those subject to "the morality of custom and the social straight-jacket" (GM II §2) (everyone) and those "definitively locked in the spell of society *and peace*'" (GM II §16; emphasis added) (priests and slaves). Whereas the warrior-nobles are able to enjoy *compensation* for the requirements of civilization by exercising their instinct for cruelty outside the bounds of society, the same does not apply to priests and slaves. Hence it is within these latter classes of person that the instinct for cruelty is turned back on itself, vents itself on itself.

This accounts for the initial form of bad conscience, bad conscience at its origins, in which it is the expression of cruelty towards the animal instincts in man, a taking pleasure in the ascetic punishment of the animal instincts, of man as an animal. As Nietzsche notes:

[This phenomenon of instincts turning back on themselves] is basically the same active force as is more impressively at work in the artists of force and organizers who build states. But here, on the inside, on a smaller, meaner scale, in the reverse direction, in the "labyrinth of the breast", to use Goethe's words, it creates for itself a bad conscience and builds negative ideals. It is that very same *instinct of freedom* (in my terminology: will to power): except that the material on which the form-creating and violating nature of this force vents itself is in this case man, the whole of his old animal self – and *not*, as is the case with that greater and more conspicuous phenomenon, the *other* man, *other* men. (GM II §18)

The emergence of bad conscience, thus, initiates the building of negative ideals in which human artistry constructs an evaluative opposition between man as a self-conscious rational being and man as an instinctual animal, directing its cruelty towards the latter and, hence, enjoying the feeling of power that comes from inflicting punishment on the animal self. It is this phenomenon of "the emergence of an animal soul turned against itself and taking sides against itself" (GM II §16) that Nietzsche takes to account for "the enigma of how contradictory concepts like *selflessness, self-denial, self-sacrifice* can suggest an ideal, a beauty" (GM II §18). As he remarks:

> One thing is certain from now on, I have no doubt – that is, the kind of pleasure the selfless, the self-denying, the self-sacrificing man feels from the outset: this pleasure belongs to cruelty. – So much provisionally on the subject of the origin of the "unegoistic" as a *moral* value and of the concealment of the ground on which this value has grown: only bad conscience, only the will to mistreat the self supplies the condition for the *value* of the unegoistic. (*Ibid.*)

If bad conscience at its origin is this "will to mistreat the self", it still remains to be explained how bad conscience is related to the feeling of guilt and, more specifically, to the moralization of the feeling of guilt that Nietzsche takes Christian morality to exhibit with regard to the interpretation of all human suffering as punishment.

Nietzsche's efforts to make this link begin with the suggestion that this "will to mistreat the self" is legitimized by reference to the creditor–debtor scheme in its religious variation; one acquires "an entitlement and right to cruelty" (GM II §5) with respect to oneself as a creaturely being in virtue of seeing oneself *qua* animal instincts as a debtor who has failed to fully repay one's debt to one's creditor, God:[5]

> Indebtedness towards *God*: this thought becomes for him an instrument of torture. In "God" he apprehends the ultimate opposing principle to his actual and irredeemable animal instincts, he himself reinterprets these animal instincts as a debt towards God (as hostility, rebellion, revolt against the "master", the "father", the original founding father and beginning of the world), he stretches himself on the rack of the contradiction between "God" and "Devil", he expels from himself every negation of himself, of nature, the natural, the reality of his being, in the form of an affirmation, as something

which exists, as incarnate, real, as God, as God's holiness, as God's judgment, as God's punishment, as the beyond, as eternity, as suffering without end, as hell, as immeasurability of punishment and guilt.   (GM II §22)

It is necessary to note at this point that in his earlier discussion of the legal system of punishment Nietzsche stressed the point that, contrary to the view that sees punishment as having "the value of awakening the *sense of guilt* in the culprit", of being "the actual *instrumentum* of the psychic reaction which is called 'bad conscience', 'pangs of conscience'", punishment, at least in this prehistorical context, "has most powerfully *hindered* the development of this sense of guilt – at least with respect to the victims on whom the power of punishment is exercised" (GM II §14). Precisely because the same type of actions that the criminal is charged with are seen by him as being practised with a good conscience by the court, Nietzsche suggests that the criminal on whom punishment descends "experienced in the process no other 'inner suffering' than he might in the event of something unexpected suddenly occurring, of a terrifying natural phenomenon, of an avalanche, against which there is no possibility of defence" (*ibid.*). (This is, incidentally, why Nietzsche suggests that the "broad effects of punishment in man and animal are increased fear, greater prudence, the mastering of desires"; GM II §15.) With the man of *bad conscience*, the will to mistreat the animal self finds expression through the religious creditor–debtor interpretation as the desire to be judged guilty and, hence, to be subject to punishment. *Punishment does not produce the sense of guilt, it vindicates the judgement that one is guilty.*

Returning to the religious context within which this development of bad conscience is worked out, Nietzsche comments:

The sense of guilt towards the divinity has continued to grow for several thousand years, and always in the same proportion as the concept and sense of God has grown and risen into the heights. ... The arrival of the Christian God, as the uttermost example of godliness so far realized on earth, has brought with it the phenomenon of the uttermost sense of guilt. Assuming that we have subsequently begun to move in the *opposite* direction, we might very probably deduce from the inexorable decline of faith in the Christian God that by now the human sense of guilt should have weakened considerably. Indeed, the prospect that the complete and definitive

victory of atheism might redeem mankind entirely from this
feeling of indebtedness towards its origins, its *causa prima*,
cannot be dismissed. Atheism and a kind of *second innocence*
belong together. (GM II §20)

However, in the next section, Nietzsche argues that this is not the case
and his reasons for making this claim introduce a new level of complexity into his argument:

> So much briefly by way of a provisional note on the relation-
> ship between religious presuppositions and the concepts of
> "guilt" and "duty". So far, I have deliberately left aside the
> actual moralization of these concepts (the way the same con-
> cepts are pushed back into the conscience; to be more pre-
> cise, the entanglement of *bad* conscience with the concept of
> God) and at the end of the previous paragraph even talked as
> if this moralization had not taken place, and, consequently,
> as if these concepts were from now on necessarily approach-
> ing their end, now that their pre-condition, the belief in our
> "creditor", in God, has collapsed. The real situation is fear-
> fully different. The moralization of the concepts guilt and
> duty, their being pushed back into *bad* conscience, actually
> represents an attempt to *reverse* the direction of the develop-
> ment just described, of at least to halt its movement.
>
> (GM II §21)

What are we to make of this passage and, in particular, Nietzsche's
remark that he has "deliberately left aside the actual moralization"
of the concepts guilt and duty? We can begin to make sense of
Nietzsche's remarks by noting that, thus far, the concept of guilt to
which he refers has the following form: the failure to keep a promise
(repay a debt) that one acknowledges the person (creditor) to whom
the promise is given (debt is owed) is entitled to expect one to keep
(repay). The sense of guilt is "a highly reflexive feeling of regret or
inadequacy at failing to honour one's obligations, which one accepts,
to a 'creditor'" (May 1999: 57). This is a moral or, if you prefer, ethical sense of guilt but it is not the "moralized" concept of guilt that
Nietzsche takes "morality" (in his specific narrow sense of this term)
to exhibit. What is the difference? What is involved in the pushing
back of this concept into bad conscience, the entanglement of bad
conscience and God?

In his discussion of the societal form of the creditor–debtor relationship, Nietzsche notes that as a community becomes stronger, they no longer take "the misdemeanours of the individual so seriously, because they no longer seem to pose the same revolutionary threat to the existence of the whole as they did previously" and suggests that this development gives rise to "the increasingly definite emergence of the will to accept every crime as in some sense capable of being *paid off*, and so, at least to a certain extent, to *isolate* the criminal from his deed" (GM II §10). For our present concerns, the crucial point concerning this development is that it creates the conceptual space needed for the slave revolt in morality, which was the subject of the first essay, and that gives rise to the fiction of the subject as one who freely chooses how to act and, hence, can be held accountable on the grounds that they could have acted differently. This is the first move in the moralization of guilt in which guilt is conceptually tied to the possibility of acting otherwise than one did. However, this expression of *ressentiment* is other-directed and the second move in the moralization of guilt is explicated in the third essay, in which, to anticipate, the elevation of the doer–deed distinction to a transcendental register and the redirecting of *ressentiment* away from others towards oneself accomplishes two things. First, one is identified oneself as the guilty agent responsible, to blame, for one's own suffering (GM III §15). Secondly, all suffering is interpreted as legitimate punishment and since human existence necessarily involves being subject to suffering in virtue of its creaturely character, one's debt can never be fully discharged without *per impossible* transcending the natural conditions of human existence; hence, human existence is itself characterized by the feeling of guilt (GM III §28). The decline of belief in God does not weaken our sense of guilt because we remain captivated by a metaphysical picture (what Nietzsche will address in the next essay as "the ascetic ideal") in which this moralized concept of guilt is held in place.

The man of bad conscience, thus, finds in "the religious presupposition" a way of giving expression to his will to mistreat the animal self that ultimately elevates this mistreatment, through the moralization of guilt, into an ideal; an ideal in which the valuing of the unegoistic and the feeling of moral guilt reach their highest pitch of intensity. This is not a necessary function of religion, as Nietzsche points out in his various references to the ancient Greeks throughout this essay. This point is most directly made in §23, in which Nietzsche notes that the fact that "the *conception* of gods" need not express such self-laceration "is revealed by the merest glance at the *Greek gods*, those reflections of noble and self-controlled man, in whom the *animal* in man felt himself deified and did *not* tear himself apart, did *not* rage against himself!" (GM II §23). Nietzsche's claim is that throughout "the longest period of their history the Greeks used their gods for no other purpose than to keep 'bad conscience' at bay, to be allowed to enjoy the freedom of their soul" (*ibid.*). This use is specifically demonstrated in how "the refined Greek" used his gods to allow for a limited separation of agent and act within the context of his commitment to an expressive picture of agency so that, confronted "with an incomprehensible atrocity and wanton crime with which one appalling crime by one of his own had tainted himself", he says:

> A *god* must have beguiled him ... This expedient is typical of the Greeks ... Thus the gods at that time served to justify man even to a certain extent in wicked actions, they served as the cause of evil – at that time they did not take upon themselves the execution of punishment, but rather, as is *nobler*, the guilt ...   (*Ibid.*)

The conception of the Greek gods is, on Nietzsche's argument, conditional on the fact that the Greeks were able to discharge their instinct for cruelty in the wilderness and, in doing so, are able to understand themselves as repaying "their founding father, their ancestors (heroes, gods) with interest, in terms of all the qualities which in the meantime have been revealed in themselves, the *noble* qualities" (GM II §19), not least by providing the gods with "*cruel* spectacles", with "*festive theatre*" (GM II §7).

Although the example of the Greeks illustrates the point that religion need not express bad conscience, we are distant from the Greeks, and the products of a history in which bad conscience has been refined and developed under the aegis of Christianity. There is no going back on this history; we cannot choose to set aside the reflectiveness that now characterizes us. At best, we can seek only to redirect bad conscience:

> to interweave bad conscience with the *unnatural* inclinations, all those aspirations to the beyond, the absurd, the anti-instinctual, the anti-animal, in short, to what have up until now been regarded as ideals, ideals which are all hostile to life, ideals that defame the world.   (GM II §24)

It is the general form of such ideals that Nietzsche will address in the third essay. Before we turn to the third essay, however, it may be worth noting that throughout the second essay Nietzsche has continued to seek to guide his readers' affective responses to "morality" through his rhetoric. Here, as in the first essay, his strategy involves contrasting the nobles (conquerors) with those enclosed with society and peace (priests and slaves) in a way that does not simply valorize the former. On the one hand, Nietzsche acknowledges that bad conscience would not have developed without the state-forming activity of those who become the nobles and, on the other hand, he stresses that bad conscience alters the aspect of the earth "as if man were not an end in himself, but rather only a pathway, an incident, a bridge, a great promise" (GM II §16) in that it develops our capacities for (and disposition to) reflection on ourselves. In this way, Nietzsche aims to bring his readers both to acknowledge an uncomfortable truth, that bad conscience emerges from, and expresses, the human instinct for cruelty, and to glimpse the possibility disclosed by the figure of the sovereign individual, that it is only as reflective and socialized creatures that we can become truly free.

It is often overlooked that in the first essay Nietzsche sets out what he takes to be "the problem of *the noble ideal itself* ... – just think *what* a problem that is: ... this synthesis of *the inhuman (Unmensch)* and *the overhuman (Übermensch)*" (GM I §16). What Nietzsche is pointing to here is the fact that the commitment to ethical autonomy exemplified by the noble ideal in its antique form was conditional on the ability of the ancient nobles to escape from the constraints of civilization in predatory warfare, and that the character of their ideal of ethical autonomy was influenced by the character of this mechanism of tension-release in that it generated a synthesis in which "consideration, self-control, tenderness, fidelity, pride and friendship" (GM I §11) (the *overhuman*) sat alongside the bestial cruelty towards foreigners (the *inhuman*), which leads Nietzsche to acknowledge that whoever met these nobles in the wild would know them only as evil enemies. In this regard, Nietzsche's sketch of the ideal of the sovereign individual as representing the form of human freedom for reflective persons socialized all the way down points to the intelligible possibility of an overcoming of the problem of the noble ideal, the possibility of a form of noble ethics in which the overhuman is no longer dependent on, and infected by, the inhuman. At the same moment that Nietzsche seeks to unsettle our image of ourselves through the figure of the man of *bad conscience*, he holds out the attraction represented by the figure of the sovereign individual.

CHAPTER SEVEN

The third essay: "What is the Meaning of Ascetic Ideals?"

The third essay, "What is the Meaning of Ascetic Ideals?", offers an analysis of the construction and power of the general form of "what have up until now been regarded as ideals, ideals which are all hostile to life, ideals that defame the world" (GM II §24). It does so by addressing "morality" under the aspect of willing in a way that accounts for the form of moral rules as categorical imperatives, that is, as universal and unconditional. Nietzsche needs to provide such an account because the first two essays do not themselves offer a sufficient explanation of these features of "morality". The first essay provides only an account of the "immanent phase" of the slave revolt and not its transcendent phase (Ridley 1998a: 41–2). The second essay points to this transcendent phase as the "moralization" of the concepts of duty and guilt, their being pushed back into bad conscience, but simply posits rather than accounts for this process. There is, moreover, a further explanatory issue that Nietzsche has yet to address, namely, how the nobles become subject to "morality", and the third essay will also address this topic.

I

We can begin by prefacing this discussion with a distinction between asceticism (i.e. ascetic procedures) and the ascetic ideal. The former refers to specific practices of self-discipline and self-constraint directed to mastering the expression of instincts and desires, and is related by Nietzsche to his discussion of punishment, internalization and the formation of a memory of the will (GM II §3). The latter denotes the idealization of asceticism as a way of life that is committed to treating living, existence itself, as an ascetic procedure whereby the end to which this procedure is directed is necessarily not immanent to existence (as with specific ascetic practices) but transcends it (GM III §11). Bearing this distinction in mind, let us turn to Nietzsche's argument.

The essay begins by considering what ascetic ideals mean in the case of the artist with some remarks on Wagner, only to conclude rapidly that ascetic ideals mean "so many things as to amount to absolutely nothing" in this case and that artists "have always acted as valets to some ethics or philosophy or religion" (GM III §5).[1] The case of Wagner and Schopenhauer is exemplary in this respect as Wagner "stood behind the philosopher Schopenhauer, as his vanguard and protection" (GM III §5). Nietzsche, thus, turns to the case of the philosopher. The contention advanced by Nietzsche is that ascetic procedures support the maximal feeling of power of philosophers in that such procedures are integral to the conditions of intellectual and spiritual living; ascetic forms of self-denial – denial of the sensual desires – serve to cultivate the philosopher's capacities for intellectual reflection and the idealization of such ascetic procedures provides a form of legitimacy for the contemplative life that enables it to persist in the face of the alternative mode of life represented by the warrior-nobles (GM III §§6–10; see also D §§18 and 42). The meaning of the ascetic ideal for the philosopher is, thus, that it enables him to affirm the value of his own existence (GM III §7). As Nietzsche remarks:

> Let us compress this whole state of affairs into a few brief phrases: in order for its existence to be *possible* at all, the philosophical spirit has at first always been obliged to disguise and mask itself in the types of contemplative man *established in earlier times*, that is, as priest, magician, prophet, above all, as a religious man. For a long time, *the ascetic ideal* has served the philosopher as a form in which to manifest himself, as a pre-condition of existence – he was obliged to *represent* it in order to be a philosopher, and he was obliged to *believe* in it in order to be able to represent it. The peculiar remoteness of the philosophers – with its negation of the world, its hostility to life, its skepticism towards the senses, its freedom from sensuality – which has survived until very recently, and in the process almost gained currency as *the philosopher's attitude* as such – this is above all a consequence of the critical situation in which philosophy first emerged and managed

to endure: that is, in so far as throughout the most of history philosophy would not have been *at all possible* on earth without an ascetic shell and disguise, without an ascetic self-misunderstanding.   (GM III §10)

The clear implication of these remarks is that the meaning of the ascetic ideal for the philosopher has been (but no longer need be) a form of justification, but also that while the philosopher may have been an advocate of the ascetic ideal, and, therefore, hardly an impartial witness as to its value, he is not its architect. On the contrary, Nietzsche's identification of the virtues of the philosopher – "his drive to doubt, his drive to negate, his drive to wait (his 'ephectic' drive), the drive to analyse, his drive to research, to seek, to dare, to compare, to balance, his will to neutrality and objectivity, his will to all *'sine ira et studio'*" – as "in contradiction with the elementary demands of morality and conscience" makes clear that, while the philosopher has required "an ascetic self-misunderstanding", the philosopher's investment in the ascetic ideal is a historically contingent rather than necessary feature of this form of life and, indeed, one that stands in tension with his strictly philosophical virtues (GM III §§9–10).[2] Nietzsche stands as his own example of how the philosophical virtues eventually break sufficiently free from the grip of the ascetic ideal to take it as an object of philosophical enquiry.

In contrast to the philosopher, the priest represents a figure whose investment in the ascetic ideal is a necessary condition of his mode of life: "This ideal constitutes not only the conviction of the ascetic priest, but also his will, his power, his interest. His *right* to exist stands and falls with this ideal" (GM III §11). It is not simply that the priest lives a contemplative mode of life and so values ascetic procedures, but that the priest "construes and uses ascetic procedures as a model for living *tout court* – as a means not merely for mastering 'something in life' but for mastering 'life itself, … its most profound, powerful, and basic conditions'" (Ridley 1998a: 66). To grasp the reason for this identification of the priest with the ascetic ideal, we need to recall, first, that the priest is a noble, that is one who understands himself as entitled to coin values, to identify his own character traits as exemplifying the good and, secondly, that the priest is subject to bad conscience, characterized by the will to mistreat his animal self. Hence, the kind of values that the priest endorses, in contrast to the warrior-noble, are those that deny the sensual and rapacious desires of humankind, for example, "poverty, humility, chastity" (GM III §8).

More generally, the priest's style of valuing is directed to the devaluation of the "powerful physicality" valued by the warrior-nobles and, in this respect, there is a degree of kinship between priestly valuations and the valuations to which the slave revolt in morality gives rise. This is not yet sufficient though to explain the priest's commitment to the ascetic ideal. The further step required involves recalling that it is not merely the case that priestly aristocratic and knightly aristocratic modes of valuation will diverge, but also, given that "the priest and warrior castes jealously confront each other and are unwilling to strike a compromise", and further that the priestly nobles are powerless in the face of the physical force that can be exercised by the warrior-nobles, the priest is, like the slave, characterized by *ressentiment* towards the knightly aristocracy (GM I §7). Unlike the slave, however, the priest is able to give expression to his desire for revenge and, in so doing, secure his own maximal feeling of power. He does so through the construction of the ascetic ideal.

At this stage, Nietzsche introduces a more precise specification of the ascetic ideal:

> The idea at issue ... is the *value* which the ascetic priests ascribe to our life: they juxtapose this life (along with all that belongs to it, "nature", "world", the whole sphere of becoming and the ephemeral) to a completely different form of existence, which it opposes and excludes, *unless* it somehow turns itself against itself, *denies itself*. In which case, the case of an ascetic life, life functions as a bridge to that other existence. The ascetic treats life as a wrong track along which one must retrace one's steps to the point at which it begins; or as a mistake which one rectifies through action – indeed, which one *should* rectify: for he *demands* that one should follow him, he imposes wherever he can his *own* evaluation of existence. (GM III §11)

This ideal offers "a closed system of will, goal and interpretation":

> The ascetic ideal has a *goal* – and this goal is sufficiently universal for all other interests of human existence to seem narrow and petty in comparison; it relentlessly interprets periods, peoples, men in terms of this goal, to allows no other interpretation, no other goal, it reproaches, negates, affirms, confirms exclusively with reference to *its* interpretation (– and has there

116

ever existed a system of interpretation more fully thought through to its end?); it subordinates itself to no other power, it believes rather in its own prerogative over all other powers, in its absolute *seniority of rank* with respect to all other powers – it believes that no power can exist on earth without first having conferred upon it a meaning, a right to existence, a value as an instrument in the service of *its* work, as a path and means to *its* goal, to its *single* goal ...   (GM III §23)

Nietzsche clarifies the sense in which this ideal is an expression of *ressentiment* by noting that it expresses "an unsatisfied instinct and will to power which seeks not to master some isolated aspect of life but rather life itself":

All this is paradoxical to an extreme: we find ourselves confronted here with a contradiction which wills itself as a contradiction, which derives *enjoyment* from this suffering and even becomes increasingly self-assured and triumphant in proportion as its own pre-condition, the physiological capacity for life, *diminishes*.   (GM III §11)

This, however, simply sharpens the issue of how the contradictory mode of life represented by the ascetic ideal can secure the revenge and maximal feeling of power of the priest. To address this issue we need to turn to the priest's reasons for proposing this ideal and the reasons why the priest's two audiences – slaves and warrior-nobles – are susceptible to it.

II

For the priest, the ascetic ideal solves two problems. The first of these problems is that concerning the relative status of knightly and priestly evaluations. The point is this: confronted by the this-worldly dominance of the knightly mode of evaluation, the ascetic ideal expresses the priest's "trumping" of this mode of evaluation through a devaluation of this-worldly existence that secures the superiority of the priestly mode of evaluation by locating the source of values in an other-worldly realm. This legitimizes the superiority of the priestly mode of valuation for the priest and, to the extent that the knightly aristocrats can be brought to accept this ideal, will also secure the this-worldly power of the priest. The second problem addressed by the priest is one that confronts the aristocratic class as a whole and concerns the fact that "a populace consumed with unresolved *ressentiment* is a dangerous, unstable, unruly populace, which it is in the interests of the higher castes to somehow subdue and keep subdued" (Ridley 1998a: 51). Following the slave revolt in morality, the slaves are characterized by a general conceptual mechanism for dealing with socially produced forms of suffering, namely identifying some agent as guilty for their suffering and thereby affirming their own value, and this, as Nietzsche points out, has the effect of ensuring that the suffering "are one and all dreadfully eager and inventive in discovering occasions for painful effects; ... they tear open their oldest wounds, they bleed from long-healed scars, they make evildoers out of their friends, wives, children, and whoever stands closest to them" (GM III §15). The problem is, thus, how to "discharge this explosive in such a way as to avoid blowing up the herd or the shepherd" (*ibid.*). It is this that the priest achieves through the ascetic ideal in that this ideal "*changes the direction of ressentiment*":

> For every suffering man instinctively seeks a cause for his suffering; more precisely, a doer, more definitely, a *guilty* doer, someone capable of suffering – in short, something living on which he can upon any pretext discharge his feelings either in fact or *in effigie*: for the discharge of feelings represents the greatest attempt on the part of the suffering man to find relief, *anaesthetic*, his involuntarily desired narcotic against pain of any sort. ... "I am suffering: someone must be to blame" – this is how all sickly sheep think. But their shepherd, the ascetic priest, tells them: "Just so, my sheep! someone must be to blame: but you yourself are this someone, you alone are to blame – *you alone are to blame for yourself!*"   (*Ibid.*)

It is clear that, if accepted by the slave, this redirecting of *ressentiment* by the ascetic priest does solve the problem confronted by the noble class, but why should this appeal to the slave? What reasons does the slave have for endorsing the ascetic ideal?

In the second essay, Nietzsche has noted what "really arouses indignation against suffering is not suffering as such but the senselessness of suffering" (GM II §7). Yet, as Ridley notes, the immanent phase of the slave revolt in morality explained in the first essay does not suffice to interpret all of the slave's suffering:

The slave has brought a certain kind and amount of suffering under a self-empowering interpretation. Most notably, because he now has the conceptual machinery required to hold the nobles accountable for oppressing him, he has brought the suffering caused by the nobles under a self-empowering interpretation. But this leaves an awful lot [of suffering] still to be accounted for. (Ridley 1998a: 42)

The salience of this fact is drawn out by Ridley as follows:

Suffering, says Nietzsche, is often "brought forward as the chief argument *against* existence"; and to the slave – a self-conscious sufferer, whose sole means of self-affirmation consists in affirming himself *through* his suffering – that argument is apt to look particularly strong. Uninterpreted suffering is fatal to him, a standing reproach not just to the manner of his existence but to the fact of it: his problem, as a self-conscious, mortal sufferer, destined for permanent repression, becomes: Why exist at all? (*Ibid*.: 43)

Precisely because the slave is denied the true reaction of deeds, he is "destined to live and die oppressed":

And death itself is a horizon for the clever man, a finality for him as it is not for the noble. The noble can *act*: he has the capacity to impose himself on the world, to leave a trace of himself, of his having existed, inscribed into it: he emerges from his depredations "convinced" that he "has provided the poets with a lot more material for song and praise". In this way, the (not too clever) noble achieves a tolerable accommodation with the prospect of his own death. Not so the slave: no one will sing of him – true deeds are denied him. When he dies, his death will be the end of him, as if he had never lived. (*Ibid*.)

The great appeal of the ascetic ideal is thus that it solves this problem for the slave by making all suffering meaningful. Since the slave is subject to bad conscience as well as *ressentiment*, this way of redirecting *ressentiment* through bad conscience so as to moralize guilt, to push it back into bad conscience, provides a mechanism for interpreting all suffering as punishment for which one is oneself (as a creaturely being characterized by sensual desires) to blame (see GM III §20). Moreover, in so interpreting suffering, the ascetic ideal provides a form of relationship to one's mortality that makes the prospect of death meaningful and, hence, bearable through an idea of immortality that is not predicated on leaving traces in the world but on transcending one's creaturely existence. In this way, the ascetic ideal seduces the suffering man to life: *"the will itself was saved"* (GM III §28).

What, though, of the warrior-nobles? Why should they be susceptible to this ideal? The ascetic priest achieved his revenge, Nietzsche writes, "once they succeeded in forcing their own misery, the whole of misery as such *into the conscience* of the fortunate: so that these latter would one day begin to feel ashamed of their good fortune" (GM III §14). But how is this achieved? In the first essay, Nietzsche suggested that "[t]he 'well-bred' *felt* themselves to be 'the fortunate'" and noted:

> If the aristocratic mode of evaluation errs and sins against reality, this happens in relation to the sphere with which it is *not* sufficiently familiar, and against real knowledge of which it stubbornly defends itself: it misjudges on occasion the sphere it despises – that of the common man, of the lower people. (GM I §10)

Nietzsche's suggestion, thus, appears to be that the knightly nobles can ward off feeling ashamed of their own good fortune to the extent that they can keep the lower peoples at epistemic arm's length. These nobles need to defend themselves against "real knowledge" of the lower people because the kind of empathetic identification with the lower orders that is a condition of such knowledge is liable to prompt questions concerning their own entitlement to good fortune. Yet, following the slave revolt in morality and the problems posed by that revolt for the noble class, it is increasingly difficult for the knightly nobles to maintain this epistemic distance. To grasp the reasons for this will require that we consider an interpretive puzzle in the *Genealogy* concerning a claim that Nietzsche makes with respect to the ascetic ideal.

The claim is that if "we put aside the ascetic ideal, then man, the *animal* man, has had no meaning up to now":

> His existence on earth has lacked a goal: "why does man exist at all?" – was a question without an answer; the *will* for man and earth was missing; behind every great human destiny

rang the even greater refrain: "In vain!" For the meaning of
the ascetic ideal is none other than *this*: that something was
missing, that man was surrounded by a gaping *void* – he did
not know how to justify, explain, affirm himself, he *suffered*
from the problem of his meaning. ... The meaningless of suffering, and *not* suffering as such, has been the curse which has
hung over mankind up to now – *and the ascetic ideal offered
mankind a meaning*! As yet, it has been the only meaning;
and any meaning is better than no meaning; in every respect,
the ascetic ideal has been the best "*faute de mieux*" so far. It
explained suffering; it seemed to fill the gaping void; the door
was closed against all suicidal nihilism. (GM III §28)

Taken at face value, this claim suggests, as Leiter has argued, that the
Greeks, too, "lacked an answer to the fundamental existential question
of, 'Suffering for *what*?'" and, hence, "had to succumb, *eventually*,
to the attractions of the ascetic ideal" (2002: 285). But it is difficult
to square this thought with the presentation of the Greeks and their
gods in the second essay, in which their religion acts to ward off bad
conscience and so support noble morality. Nietzsche remarks:

The aspect of suffering which actually causes outrage is not
suffering itself, but the meaninglessness of suffering: but neither the Christian who has interpreted a whole secret machinery of salvation into suffering, nor for the naïve man of earlier
times, who knew how to interpret all suffering in relation to
those who actually inflict it or view it as spectacle, did such a
meaningless suffering actually exist. So that hidden, undiscov-
ered and unwitnessed suffering could be banished from the
world and honestly negated, mankind was virtually forced to
invent gods and supernatural beings of all heights and depths
– ... In any case, it is certain that even the *Greeks* knew no
more pleasant seasoning for the happiness of the gods than
the joys of cruelty. With what eyes, then, do you think Homer
let his gods gaze down upon the fates of men? What ultimate
meaning did Trojan Wars and similar fearful tragedies have?
There is absolutely no doubt about it: they were intended as
festive theatre for the gods ... (GM II §7)

But if we reject Leiter's proposal, can we make sense of Nietzsche's
claim? Perhaps one way to do so is to note that the Greek's way of

dealing with the threat of suicidal nihilism cannot act as a general solution to this threat, a solution for man as such, but only as a solution for the Greek nobles and this presents a problem for the Greek nobles in that to the extent that they cannot provide an answer to the question "Suffering for *what*?" that has general appeal, the problem of explosive *ressentiment* remains unresolved. Interpreting their suffering as providing a spectacle for the gods is, after all, not sufficient to provide the slave with a reason to exist precisely on the grounds offered by Ridley and cited above; only those who can grasp immortality in terms of having inscribed their existence through deeds into the world are liable to see this festive interpretation of suffering as sufficing.

How does this bear on the issue of the knightly noble's ability to maintain epistemic distance with respect to the slaves? Since the problem of explosive *ressentiment* is a problem for the noble class as a whole and one that requires the "real knowledge" of the slave provided by the ascetic priest, then the knightly noble has reason to endorse the priest's solution to this problem but such endorsement entails a lessening of the epistemic distance between noble and slave, and hence an exposure to the kind of demands for reasons involved in the ascetic ideal, a demand for reasons that are metaphysical rather than mythological, that is, reasons that do not simply express aspects of the ethical culture in terms of which the knightly nobles understand their own activity but justify that ethical background itself.[3] To the extent that this new kind of demand for reasons gets a grip on the warrior nobles in virtue of the lessening of their epistemic distance from the slave, it is liable to prompt just that form of questioning – for example, "What right do I have to be fortunate?" – to which the knightly worldview is itself unable to respond and, hence, renders the knight susceptible to the one framework within which such questions can be engaged: the ascetic ideal (see Migotti 1998). Nietzsche suggests in his discussion of this topic in "The Problem of Socrates" in *Twilight of the Idols* and in *The AntiChrist* that this demand for reasons only takes hold under conditions in which the existing mythological structure is already under various kinds of pressure but, be that as it may, this account provides an explanation of why the noble is, eventually, attracted to the ascetic ideal that is consonant with Nietzsche's insistence on the claim that the ascetic ideal is the only general mechanism for solving the problem of the meaning of suffering thus far.

If cogent, Nietzsche's argument thus far serves to establish that the ascetic ideal is a mechanism through which the priest secures his revenge and maximal feeling of power. More generally, Nietzsche has shown that the ascetic ideal acts to secure the conditions of human willing by providing a general answer to the question "Suffering for *what*?" Its conditional value consists in just this. The mode of willing that it secures is "a *will to nothingness*, an aversion to life, a rebellion against the most fundamental pre-conditions of life" but it "is and remains none the less a *will*!" (GM III §28). Furthermore, his account of the general form of the ascetic ideal as involving a devaluation of this-worldly existence that situates the source of value in another metaphysical realm offers an account of how "morality" comes to be characterized by a view of values as unconditioned and of moral rules as unconditional commands. However, two further features of Nietzsche's argument in this essay remain to be addressed.

The first addresses the fact that the ascetic ideal derives its power not merely from the fact that it is the only general answer to the problem of suffering thus far but also from the fact that it presents itself as objectively valid, that is, as the only possible way of conceptualizing human existence. It is this in-built denial of its own perspectival character that, on Nietzsche's account, explains how we have come to be wholly captivated by the way of reflecting and evaluating human existence expressed in the ascetic ideal. Consequently Nietzsche needs both to show how the ascetic ideal gives rise to a picture of knowing that supports this claim and to undermine this picture.

The second concerns the relationship between the ascetic ideal and the will to truth, that is, that very truthfulness that Nietzsche appeals to in advancing his arguments concerning "morality" and the need for a re-evaluation of values. In particular, Nietzsche takes it to be necessary to address the claim that science represents a rival to the ascetic ideal in order to demonstrate to his audience that the movement in which he takes them to participate from a religious to a scientific worldview does not itself denote the displacement of the ascetic ideal. Indeed, it is in respect of this issue that the opening arguments of the third essay may be calculated to mislead because, on the surface, they construct a distinction between the religious and the secular, the transcendent and the immanent, that give rise the appearance that honest atheism is a counter to the illusions of the ascetic ideal. In taking up the case of science, Nietzsche will cut away the ground beneath such an appealing and reassuring thought.[4]

III

The first of these topics arises as Nietzsche considers the question of the kind of philosophical outlook to which the ascetic ideal gives rise. Central to such a philosophical perspective is the metaphysical distinction between "real" and "apparent" worlds, the history of which Nietzsche will later critically sketch in "How the 'Real World' at last became a Myth" in *Twilight of the Idols*. His main focus in this passage, however, is the kind of epistemological picture that emerges within this metaphysical perspective and its exemplification of the paradoxical and self-contradictory character of the ascetic ideal. The salient remarks are these:

> From now on, my dear philosophers, let us beware of the dangerous old conceptual fable which posited a "pure, will-less, painless, timeless knowing subject", let us beware of the tentacles of such contradictory concepts as "pure reason", "absolute spirituality", "knowledge in itself"; – for these always ask us to imagine an eye which is impossible, an eye which supposedly looks out in no particular direction, an eye which supposedly either restrains or altogether lacks the active powers of interpretation which first makes seeing into seeing something – for here, then, a nonsense and non-concept is demanded of the eye. Perspectival seeing is the *only* kind of seeing there is, perspectival "knowing" the *only* kind of "knowing": and the *more* feelings about a matter which we allow to come to expression, the *more* eyes, different eyes through which we are able to view this same matter, the more complete our "conception" of it, our "objectivity", will be. But to eliminate the will completely, to suspend the affects altogether, even assuming that we could do so: what? Would this not amount to the *castration* of the intellect?   (GM III §12)

These remarks are concisely directed at the accounts of the nature of knowers, of knowledge and the objects of knowledge invoked by the epistemological expression of the ascetic ideal.

First, to conceptualize knowers "as 'pure, will-less, painless, timeless, knowing' subjects, is to extrude from them precisely those embedded and embodied features that make knowing possible at all" (Ridley 2000: 92). Even if we could suspend our affects, the result would be to castrate the intellects "because among the 'affects' to be suspended would be the desire to know (the will to truth) and the desire to produce rationally acceptable explanations of the phenomena we know about" (*ibid.*):

> To suspend these would be to leave behind only the "nonsensical absurdity" of "contemplation without interest", i.e., of contemplation somehow conducted in the absence even of our cognitive interests (in things like simplicity, explanatory power, etc.), let alone those other interests (in things like convenience, survival, etc.) that give us reasons for wanting to know anything in the first place. (*Ibid.*)

In contrast to this self-contradictory picture, Nietzsche's account presents the knower as a natural creature situated "in the interstices of those patterns of interest and desire that he calls 'system[s] of purposes'. This is what it is for a knower to have a 'perspective'; and perspective is an essential prerequisite of knowing" (*ibid.*).

Secondly, the ascetic ideal's self-contradictory account of knowers dovetails with a paradoxical account of knowledge as perspectiveless, as knowledge in itself, as Truth, rather than acknowledging that "because generated by knowers whose perspectives are defined by particular systems of purposes, knowledge is always a function of the interests immanent to those systems" (*ibid.*: 93).

Thirdly, these two features of the epistemological picture cultivated by the ascetic ideal produce an equally self-contradictory and paradoxical account of the object of knowledge:

> If we had no interests or purposes, no perspective, objects would be encountered in no terms at all, and so would not, in nay intelligible sense, be encountered. It is for this reason that Nietzsche is so scathing about the Kantian "thing-in-itself", the elusive essence of an object that supposedly underlies its "mere" appearance. "[W]hat could I say", Nietzsche asks, "about any essence except to name the attributes of its appearance! Certainly ... [an appearance is] not a mask that one could place on an unknown X or remove from it!" This, in Nietzsche's view, the very idea of a "thing-in-itself" – of an essence, an "unknown X" – to which appearances somehow accrue, is unintelligible, "a *contradictio in adjecto*", since the subtraction from a thing of all its possible appearances simply constitutes the subtraction of the thing itself. (*Ibid.*)

Rather, it is only through perspective that "seeing something becomes seeing *something*", that is, we encounter objects in terms set by our systems of purposes; the objects of knowledge:

> are just objects: things singled out as such as a result of the ways in which they impinge on various systems of purposes, and conceived in terms set by those systems. Which is why Nietzsche insists that "the *more* eyes, different eyes, we can use to observe one thing, the more complete will our 'concept' of this thing, our 'objectivity', be".   (*Ibid.*: 93–4)

The purposes of this concise critical argument concerning the epistemological picture are threefold: first, to demonstrate its self-contradictory character; secondly, to make the point that the incoherence of this epistemological picture is an exemplary expression of the self-contradictory and paradoxical character of the ascetic ideal itself in which a perspective is driven to deny its own perspectival character; and thirdly, to contrast this epistemological picture with the naturalized epistemology of perspectivism in order to release us from the grip of the picture and to account for the form of "objectivity" exhibited by Nietzsche's genealogical essays, in which an object of knowledge – "morality" – is addressed from a variety of perspectives.

IV

The second topic that remains to be addressed is Nietzsche's turn, following §23, to consider the relationship of science to the ascetic ideal. Thus far Nietzsche has both explained the power of the ascetic ideal as the only general answer to the problem of the meaning of suffering and argued for the self-contradictory character of the ascetic ideal. What he has not done is provide his audience with the right kind of reason, a reason expressing an intrinsic value within "morality", for rejecting the ascetic ideal. Moreover, since the arguments of both of the first two essays of the *Genealogy* could be accepted, at least in principle, by scientific atheists, then in the light of his claim that the ascetic ideal is the only general ideal so far, Nietzsche needs to make clear why he does not take science (or, more accurately, as we shall see, scientism) to be a rival to the ascetic ideal but the most honest and noble expression of it and, hence, of "morality".

Nietzsche's contention is that his scientific contemporaries are characterized by a:

> stoicism of the intellect which renounces negation with the same severity as affirmation, the desire to stop short at the factual, the *factum brutum* ... in which French science is now seeking a kind of moral superiority over German science, the complete renunciation of interpretation ... [and that] what *compels* these men to this absolute will to truth, albeit as its unconscious imperative, is the *belief in the ascetic ideal itself* – make no mistake on this point – it is the belief in a *metaphysical* value, the value of *truth in itself*, as it alone is guaranteed and attested in each ideal (it stands of falls with each ideal).
>
> (GM III §24)

His argument for this claim begins with the following point:

> Strictly speaking, there is absolutely no science "without pre-suppositions", the very idea is inconceivable, paralogical: a philosophy, a "belief" must always exist first in order for science to derive from it a direction, a meaning, a limit, a method, a *right* to existence.
>
> (GM III §24)

Science, in other words, cannot itself ground its own value: provide an answer to the question as to why scientific knowledge is worth knowing. This is no objection to science but merely a restatement of the point that scientific knowledge is bound up with our interest and desires, our systems of purposes. However, when science denies its perspectival character, denies its standing as one (set of) way(s) of encountering and interpreting the world among others, and presents itself as a perspectiveless take on how the world really is, as "the true account of the world", that is, when belief in science becomes scientism in the way that Nietzsche takes to be true of his contemporaries, then this belief in science stands as an expression of the ascetic ideal. It does so because science, so conceived, expresses an unconditional will to truth, to "the value of *truth in itself*", that is, it posits Truth "as an unconditionally valuable goal whose pursuit is metaphysically self-justifying" (Ridley 2000: 96). And this is to say that the scientist faith in science:

> *affirms in the process another world* from that of life, nature and history; and in so far as he affirms this "other world",

> what? must he not then in the process – deny its counterpart,
> this world, *our* world? ... The belief upon which our science
> rests remains a *metaphysical belief.* (GM III §24)

So much for the claim that scientism is a rival to the ascetic ideal. As Nietzsche puts it: "this *remnant* of the ideal, is, if one is willing to believe me, the strictest, most spiritual formulation of the ideal itself, absolutely esoteric, stripped of all outworks – not so much its remnant, then, as its *core*" (GM III §27).

However, in making it plain that the unconditional will to truth expressed in our faith in science is an expression of the ascetic ideal, Nietzsche also provides the grounds for offering his audience a reflectively stable reason for "overcoming" the ascetic ideal, namely, that it is this very unconditional will to truth cultivated by the ascetic ideal that ultimately exposes its incoherence. It is our commitment to truthfulness that leads us, and Nietzsche's own philosophical development exemplifies this process, to reject the metaphysical claim for the unconditional value of truth and to acknowledge that truth is bound to immanent systems of purposes and, hence, that the value of truth is conditional: a function of the value of those systems of purposes. In a passage of considerable rhetorical force, Nietzsche attempts to implicate his audience in this process in which our commitment to truthfulness – a product of "Christian morality itself, the increasing seriousness with which truthfulness was taken, the refinement of the Christian conscience in confession, translated and sublimated into the scientific conscience, into intellectual hygiene at all costs" (*ibid.*; cf. GS §357) – is leading to the self-overcoming of the ascetic ideal:

> In this way, Christianity *as dogma* was destroyed by its own
> morality; in this way Christianity *as morality* must now be
> destroyed – we are standing on the threshold of *this* very
> event. After Christian truthfulness has drawn one conclusion
> after another, it finally draws its strongest *conclusion*, its con-
> clusion *against* itself; this will occur when it asks the question:
> "*What is the meaning of all will to truth?*" (GM III §27)

Nietzsche's *Genealogy* is itself situated by these remarks as an event within this process, as a contribution of truthfulness to the destruction of Christian morality, whose meaning and value are given by the system of purposes that it serves: the need for a re-evaluation of values. If, as Nietzsche has argued, the ascetic ideal is incoherent, then we can no longer understand ourselves as ethical agents within the terms of "morality" nor retreat to the standpoint of scientism, for that standpoint too remains within the ambit of the ascetic ideal; on the contrary, we are *compelled* by a reason deriving from the core of "morality" to engage in the project of re-evaluation to which Nietzsche enjoins us.

V

We are now in a position to grasp the force of the question raised by Nietzsche in the preface to this work, where he writes:

> What if there existed a symptom of regression in the "good man", likewise, a danger, a temptation, a poison, a narcotic, by means of which the present were living *at the expense of the future*? Perhaps more comfortably and less dangerously, but also in less grand style, in a humbler manner? ... So that none other than morality itself would be the culprit, if the *highest power and splendour* of the human type, in itself a possibility, were never to be reached? So that morality would constitute the danger of dangers? (GM Preface §6)

In the light of Nietzsche's arguments in the *Genealogy*, the concerns expressed in this passage can be understood as fourfold. First, "morality" commits us to a view of ourselves in which agency is understood in the non-expressive terms of a unitary subject of free will and, hence, distorts our understanding of the nature of our own agency; it presents a picture of our moral agency in terms of an incoherent notion of the voluntary such that the feeling of power has no necessary relationship to our actual powers of agency. Secondly, "morality" obstructs the development of human powers of ethical reflection and evaluation in that it presents moral values as unconditioned and, hence, as independent of us. To the extent that we remain held captive by this perspective, "morality" cannot itself be taken as an object of critical appraisal and, thereby, blocks the development of our powers of critical appraisal. Thirdly, precisely because "morality", at root, expresses a will to nothingness, it generates a feeling of power by directing our agency towards the illusory and impossible goal of transcending the conditions of human agency. Fourthly, to the extent that "morality" is undermined by its own will to truth, this raises the spectre of nihilism.

We can develop this final point further by noting that Nietzsche argues that the self-destruction of the ascetic ideal threatens to undermine our capacities for "self-discipline", "self-surveillance", "self-overcoming" (GM III §16) and our disposition to truthfulness precisely because we now lack an overarching goal in the service of which these capacities and this disposition are cultivated. But this undermining does not entail any diminution of our dissatisfaction with our worldly existence. The suffering endemic to life itself remains; all that has gone is the (ascetic) mode of valuing that rendered such suffering meaningful, and hence bearable. Thus Nietzsche discerns the outlines of a creature whose best capacities have atrophied and whose relationship to its own existence is one of perpetual dissatisfaction. The threat here is obvious:

> What is to be feared, what has a more calamitous effect than any other calamity, is that man should inspire not profound fear but profound *nausea*; also not great fear but great *pity*. Suppose these two were one day to unite, they would inevitably beget one of the uncanniest monsters: the "last will" of man, his will to nothingness, nihilism. And a great deal points to this union. (GM III §14)

Nietzsche's critique of morality is, finally, a response to this threat.

CHAPTER EIGHT

Debating the *Genealogy*

In the light of the foregoing analyses, we are now in a position to comprehend the overall argumentative strategy of the *Genealogy* as a critical re-evaluation of "morality" in which Nietzsche attempts to free us from the grip of "morality", our captivation by "morality", such that it becomes an object that can be subjected to critical appraisal and evaluation, to provide us with internal reasons for rejecting "morality" and to mobilize our existing affective dispositions against "morality". Each of the essays seeks to loosen the grip of "morality" by providing a psychologically realistic account of the formation of its central features, which, in virtue of its naturalistic form, undermines the self-understanding of "morality" and which, in virtue of its psychological content, mobilizes our affective dispositions against "morality". Moreover, in a somewhat loose sense, these three essays sketch a narrative in which the second essay provides a naturalistic account of how we come to be creatures who stand (and must stand) in evaluative relationships to ourselves and the world, the first essay provides an account of how the different social and political conditions within which we are situated give rise to different forms of ethical reasoning and the third essay indicates how we have come to be held captive by a particular kind of ethical reasoning: "morality". This raises the question of why the first and second essays are presented in the order that they are. On the account I have offered, Nietzsche has a principled reason to offer them in this order, namely, that the first essay, by presenting "morality" as slave morality, as a counter-movement to, and re-evaluation of, noble morality, immediately and dramatically problematizes the presumption of his audience that "morality" is the only possible ethical perspective in making visible another mode of ethical reasoning and rhetorically situating the reader within the struggle between them, while also indicating that the enterprise of re-evaluation to which he enjoins his readers is not a novel phenomenon.

But as I indicated in Chapter 4, this account of genealogy as a form of critical reflection is by no mean uncontroversial; in this chapter I shall defend it in relation to Nietzsche's *Genealogy* against three rival accounts offered by Leiter, (later) Geuss and Williams. In each case, the precise issue at stake is somewhat different and, consequently, I shall address each in turn.

I

To situate Leiter's argument appropriately, it will be useful to deploy a set of distinctions concerning the value of values and the possible forms that the activity of re-evaluation may take that have been drawn by Ridley. First, Ridley proposes that Nietzsche's understanding of the (conditional) value of values can be grasped in terms of the construal of values either as instrumentally valuable or as intrinsically valuable:

> Something has *direct instrumental value* ... if its value resides chiefly in its being a means to some kind of (valuable) end. ... Something has *indirect instrumental value*, by contrast, if its value resides chiefly in its promoting or making more likely the realization of some kind of (valuable) end, even though it does not function directly as a means to that end. ... Instrumental value, whether direct or indirect, is thus conditional upon the fact of ends which are themselves valuable. Such ends are treated by Nietzsche as intrinsically valuable, where something has *intrinsic value* if, given what else is the case, its value does not reside chiefly in being a means or an enabling factor towards some further kind of (valuable) end. Intrinsic value is thus conditional upon facts – natural, social, practical or cultural – that are or might be peculiar to particular ways of living, as well as (often) upon the relations of value in question to the other values have a place in some particular way of life. ... A value is intrinsically valuable with a respect to a given way of living if, other things being equal, it can, by itself, *motivate* ... (Ridley 2005: 174)[1]

Secondly, on the basis of these distinctions, Ridley proposes five ways in which a value (or set of values) might be subject to re-evaluation:

1. Showing that V, although an intrinsic value, is indirectly instrumental in realising ends said to be bad, although not ends that could be acknowledged as "bad" from the standpoint of the relevant way of living.

2. Showing that V, although an intrinsic value, is indirectly instrumental in realising a good end from the standpoint of the relevant way of living.

3. Showing that V is indeed an intrinsic value for a given way of living, but not one held in place by the reasons or other values that are usually supposed.

4. Showing that V is indeed an intrinsic value, but is held in place by reasons or other values that, from the standpoint of the relevant way of living, are bad.

5. Showing that V, although an instrinsic value, or a set of intrinsic values, is indirectly instrumental in realizing ends that can, in principle, be grasped as bad from the standpoint of the relevant way of living. (*Ibid.*: 177–8)[2]

For Leiter, Nietzsche's *Genealogy* is an example of 1. Leiter's claim is that Nietzsche re-evaluates "morality" by showing that the values of "morality" are indirectly instrumental in obstructing or suppressing the realization of human excellence, where "human excellence" is construed in terms of what Nietzsche takes to have intrinsic value. On this interpretation, Nietzsche's genealogy of "morality" confronts the problem of authority: why, precisely, should the fact that "morality" suppresses the emergence of what Nietzsche regards as human excellence be seen as a problem from the point of view of those who do not share this conception of human excellence? Leiter's response to this problem is to argue that the philosophical function of genealogy, for Nietzsche, is directed to freeing "nascent higher beings from their false consciousness" about "morality", "their false belief that ["morality"] is *good for them*" (Leiter 2002: 176). And, hence, to argue that the problem of authority does not arise since Nietzsche's intended audience is circumscribed "to those who share Nietzsche's evaluative taste, those for whom no justification would be required: those who are simply 'made for it,' 'whose ears are related to ours,' who are 'predisposed and predestined' for Nietzsche's insights" (*ibid.*: 150). This is, as Ridley notes "a somewhat desperate tactic" and it "is also a tactic that collapses" since Leiter's view that Nietzsche's rhetoric is designed to shake his (select) audience out of their intuitive commitment to "morality" rather "indicates that the members of Nietzsche's 'proper' audience are not 'predisposed' to accept the authority of his evaluative standpoint after all" (Ridley 2005: 180). It is a measure of the lengths to which Leiter is forced to go to maintain this account that he is constrained to argue that Nietzsche's appeal to the value of truthfulness is not a form of internal criticism of "morality" because the will to truth represents a standpoint "which is *not* internal to Christian morality, but which Christian morality helped produce" (Leiter 2002: 175 n.7). This is, to put it mildly, hard to square with Nietzsche's claim in *The Gay Science* §344 that with our commitment to the uncondional will to truth "*we stand on moral ground*" and, equally, with the *Genealogy*, third essay, §27. In contrast, and accepting Ridley's claim that all of 2–5 may be found in the *Genealogy*, the reading that I have offered makes it clear the main form of re-evaluation in which Nietzsche engages is Ridley's proposal 5 (itself only a deeper version of 4), in which it is on the basis of our commitment to truthfulness that we can come to recognize that "morality" "has the effect of making us obscure to ourselves, or – which is a different way of saying the same thing – has the effect of inhibiting our capacity to experience ourselves, fully, as agents" (Ridley 2005: 188). To the extent that we are truthful, Nietzsche's argument goes, we are constrained to recognize that we can no longer make sense of ourselves as ethical beings in terms of "morality" and, hence, possess an internal reason to reject "morality".

II

The issue with respect to Geuss's view of genealogy is somewhat different. Recall that Geuss makes the following claim:

> To be sure, a genealogy *can* undermine various *beliefs* about the origin of different forms of valuation. If I have a certain form of valuation I may need to believe certain things – if I am a Christian I may need to believe certain things about the origin of Christian valuation. So if those beliefs are undermined, I may feel my values undermined, too, but this is as it were *my* problem, not part of the intention of genealogy.
> (Geuss 1999a: 20)

He continues:

> It is a particular and idiosyncratic problem of Christianity that it cultivates truthfulness and introspection and is a form of valuation which requires its devotees to make claims and have beliefs that won't stand up to truthful introspective scrutiny (such as that moral action arises from altruistic sources). This means that Christianity will dissolve itself and Nietzsche's genealogy will contribute to that process. That genealogy is experienced by the Christian as a form of criticism need not imply that that is how it looks from the perspective of genealogists themselves. *(Ibid.*: 21)

There are two problems with this argument. The first, and more minor, problem is that Geuss limits Nietzsche's target audience to Christians (by which he means those who believe in Christianity). While Christians are certainly a part of the audience being addressed, it is hard to see why Geuss should imagine that Nietzsche's arguments do not equally apply to atheists such as those described in *The Gay Science* §125, who accept Christian morality while rejecting Christian religious beliefs and, indeed, those who are committed to scientism and are addressed in the third essay. On the reconstruction that I have proposed, Nietzsche is concerned to offer internal reasons to reject "morality" to all of these groups, that is, to the entire body of his contemporaries. The second, and more significant, problem concerns the argument that the fact that genealogy undermines Christian valuations is an incidental rather than integral feature of genealogy. Geuss's claim is sustainable in some respects in that the genealogist does not have to be committed to the view that *ressentiment*, cruelty and partiality are bad and hence that what is experienced as criticism by the Christian in these respects need not look like that from the standpoint of the genealogist. But this claim, which itself seems to underestimate the complexity of Nietzsche's argumentative strategy since, as Janaway has stressed, it is part of the intention of Nietzsche's genealogy to mobilize the affects of his audience against "morality", cannot be sustained with respect to truthfulness since truthfulness (on my account) also functions as an intrinsic (but not unconditional) value for Nietzsche and, consequently, the fact that "Christianity is a tissue of lies" is, *contra* Geuss, a fact of critical evaluative significance for Nietzsche as well as for Christians.

Geuss advances this claim with respect to truthfulness because he holds that Nietzsche "has no objection to lying *per se*, but only to those forms of lying that in fact sap human vitality, turn the will against itself, denigrate life, or stunt 'the growth of the plant "man"'" (Geuss 1999a: 21). However, while it is true that Nietzsche does object to these forms of lying and it is also true that the fact that he takes truth to be a conditional value entails that there can, in principle, be justifiable ("noble") lies, it is less clear that he objects *only* to these forms of lying. Rather, I suggest, Nietzsche is committed to the view that lying is bad except where the value of truth is trumped by other intrinsic values. The disagreement between Geuss's view and my own account is, thus, that whereas he holds that Nietzsche is committed to the view that truth is only instrumentally valuable, I claim that Nietzsche takes truth to be intrinsically (but not unconditionally) valuable. It is, moreover, precisely because Geuss holds this view that he also claims that the fact (if it is one) that Nietzsche's genealogy gives "an historically more accurate and plausible account of our Christian morality from the standpoint of his own new positive valuation of life than Christians themselves can from the standpoint of their ascetic ideals" (*ibid.*) can yield, at best, only indirect support for Nietzsche's perspective. Now, apart from the point already stressed in Chapter 2 that Nietzsche's account can only have the right kind of reflective stability if truth is an intrinsic value within his perspective, we may also note two further considerations in support of the view that Nietzsche holds truth to be an intrinsic, rather than instrumental, value. The first is that this view fits much more easily with Nietzsche's argument that truthfulness or, more precisely, *redlichkeit* is a virtue, indeed, *the* virtue of "free spirits" and "immoralists" such as himself:

> Genuine honesty [*Redlichkeit*], assuming that this is our virtue and we cannot get rid of it, we free spirits – well then, we will want to work on it with all the love and malice at our disposal, and not get tired of "perfecting" ourselves in *our* virtue, the only one we have left: may its glory come to rest like a gilded, blue evening glow of mockery over this aging culture and its dull and dismal seriousness! And if our genuine honesty nevertheless gets tired one day and sighs and stretches its limbs and finds us too harsh and would rather say things that were better, easier, gentler like an agreeable vice: we will stay *harsh*, we who are the last of the Stoics! And we will help it out with what ever devilishness we have – our disgust at clumsiness and approximation, our "*nitimur in vetitum*," our adventurer's courage, our sly and discriminating curiosity,

> our subtlest, most hidden, most spiritual will to power and
> world-overcoming, which greedily rambles and raves over
> every realm of the future, – we will bring all of our "devils"
> to help out our "god"!   (BGE §227)

The second is that when Nietzsche talks of justified falsification with respect to ourselves, he makes it clear that falsification is justified only in so far as it is a necessary condition of being able to endure one's life. As Ridley remarks, commenting on *The Gay Science* §290 ("One Thing is Needful"), in which Nietzsche speaks of the necessity of giving style to one's character, Nietzsche's point in this passage is that "*every* character needs sooner or later to deceive itself, and Nietzschean truthfulness can only be taken so far, no matter how much strength of spirit one has" and hence "the last role of truthfulness is truthfully to surrender to the necessity of deceiving oneself, having stood firm against one's heart's desire to capitulate sooner" (Ridley 1998a: 140). As Ridley continues: "Style, on this reading, is not so much a matter of opportunistic self-exculpation as the (honest) last resort of a soul that can face no more" (*ibid.*; see also GS §107). In the light of the considerations, it is reasonable to conclude that Nietzsche, for all that he acknowledges that there is "no pre-established harmony between the furtherance of truth and the well-being of mankind" (HAH §517), is committed to the intrinsic value of truth.

It thus follows, *contra* Geuss's claim that Nietzsche's genealogy supplies his readers with no reasons to embrace Nietzsche's own perspective, that this is precisely what the *Genealogy* does accomplish in guiding its audience, first, to the recognition that they can no longer truthfully make sense of themselves as moral agents in terms of "morality" and, secondly, to the acknowledgment that Nietzsche's perspective provides a way in which they can make sense of this phenomenon and, hence, of themselves as beings fated to re-evaluate their values.

In their different ways, the problems of the accounts offered by Leiter and Geuss both stem from the fact that they fail to grasp that Nietzsche's critical re-evaluation of morality is articulated through a commitment to the intrinsic value of truth shared by Nietzsche and his audience. Thus, on Leiter's account, genealogy becomes boring, a crude and probably incoherent exercise in ideology-critique; while, on Geuss's account, genealogy ceases to be a re-evaluation at all. In contrast, on the account that I have offered, Nietzsche's development of genealogy as a mode of enquiry is an exercise in internal criticism that seeks both to undermine "morality" and to demonstrate the superiority of the naturalistic perspective of will to power in terms that all those subject to "morality" could in principle accept.

III

What, though, of the critical force of Nietzsche's genealogy? Is it dependent on the historical truth of his accounts? Addressing this question involves starting with a prior question: are his genealogical accounts to be regarded as historical at all? This question arises because it has been argued that Nietzsche's accounts are best read, even if not entirely intended, as fictions (May 1999: 52; Williams 2000: 157–61). This argument has been most cogently advanced by Williams and so it is with discussion of his defence of this claim that we shall begin.

Williams's discussion of genealogy, and Nietzsche's *Genealogy* in particular, situates it within the broader context of a discussion of a non-reductive naturalism about ethics, that is, a naturalism that seeks as far as possible to account for our current ethical psychology in terms ultimately drawn from other aspects of human psychology. In this context, Williams argues that fictional developmental stories can "explain how" concepts or values or institutions "can emerge and provide new reasons for action" and do so "in terms of existing reasons for action" such that "the new reasons for action stand in a rational or intelligible relation to original reasons or motivations" (2000: 156). Turning to Nietzsche's *Genealogy*, which Williams characterizes as having "the property of being at once extremely compelling, in particular because it seems to hit on something with great exactitude, and at the same time of being infuriatingly vague" (*ibid.*: 157), he makes the following claim:

> Now Nietzsche himself gives us, centrally to his story, a phe-nomenological representation, which seems to represent a psychological process leading from the earlier ethical condi-tion [the condition prior to the slave revolt in morality] to something like to the outlook in the later ethical condition (the explanandum) [the condition of slave morality]. If this were a psychological process, it should be recognizable in an individual. But an actual process that led to the actual expla-nadum could not happen in an individual, since the outcome consists of socially legitimated beliefs, and they could not be merely the sum of individual fantasies. Rather, this is a social process which in actual fact no doubt has many stages,

discontinuities and contingencies, but which – the idea is – can be illuminatingly represented on the model of a certain kind of psychological strategy.   (*Ibid.*: 156)

This leads Williams to construe Nietzsche's genealogy in the following terms: "A fictional story which represents a new reason for action as being developed in a simplified situation as a function of motives, reactions, psychological processes which we have reason to acknowledge already" (*ibid.*: 159). His point is that this fictional genealogical account presses the question as to:

whether one could understand the explanandum in terms of the fictional history and still (more or less) accept in their original terms the reasons for action which the explanandum provides. In the example of [the *Genealogy*], the phenomenological fiction of *ressentiment* does not permit this: once again, this is a result of the special demands of ["morality"], that it should present itself as separate from and higher than such motives. This expresses its deep involvement in what Nietzsche called "the metaphysicians basic belief, *the belief in the opposition of values*".   (*Ibid.*: 159–60)

Williams recognizes that this construal of Nietzsche's account does raise a specific instance of "the general question of how explanation in terms of a fictional story can be explanation at all, or do anything for our understanding of the actual" and restricts himself to:

saying only that to the extent such stories do succeed in relating a value which gives us some reasons for action to other reasons for action which, as I very roughly put it, we have "anyway", to that extent there will be a question – one might say, a relevant thought experiment – of whether we could, if we knew such a story to be true, go on giving the derived value the kind of respect we give it.   (*Ibid.*: 160)

It should also be noted that Williams does not argue that Nietzsche's *Genealogy* is simply fictional:

Nietzsche's genealogy is by no means meant to be entirely fictional. It has something to do with history, although it is far from clear what history: there are some vaguely situated

> masters and slaves; then an historical change, which has some-
> thing to do with Jews or Christians; there is a process which
> culminates perhaps in the Reformation, perhaps in Kant. It
> has been going on for two thousand years.　　　(*Ibid.*: 37)

However, it seems clear that its relationship to history is part of what
makes the *Genealogy* "infuriatingly vague" for Williams, whereas it is
its fictions that "hit on something with great exactitude".

The value of Williams's discussion is twofold. First, it makes clear
that Nietzsche's *Genealogy* can play a critical role even if it is entirely
fictional. Secondly, it draws attention to a central feature of Nietzsche's
rhetorical and argumentative strategy, namely, the presentation of
sociohistorical processes of belief formation and legitimation through
the device of human types (e.g. the priest, the knight, the slave). With
respect to the first of these points, Williams's position is surely right,
yet it is far from clear that the critical role that the *Genealogy* can play
if fictional is the critical role that Nietzsche, on the account I have
offered, designs it to play. The role Williams assigns the *Genealogy* is,
I think, too weak since Nietzsche is not simply concerned to raise – as,
say, "a relevant thought experiment" – a question concerning "whether
we could, if we knew such a story to be true, go on giving the derived
value the kind of respect we give it" (*ibid.*: 160) but, rather, to compel
us to recognize that, if his account is true, we cannot go on understanding ourselves, being intelligible to ourselves as ethical agents, in terms
of "morality". However, the more important point for this discussion
concerns Williams's argument for the fictional status of Nietzsche's
genealogical account; the relevant question is whether Nietzsche's use
of the dramatic device of human types as a way of presenting and con-
ducting his argument implies that his account is fictional as opposed
to historical in character.

There are a number of reasons to doubt this claim. On textual
grounds, one can note Nietzsche's affirmation that his genealogy is
directed to presenting "the real *history of morality*" in contrast to
"English hypothesizing *into the blue*":

> For there is clearly another colour which ought to be a hun-
> dred times more important to a genealogist of morals: that
> is, *grey* – by that I mean what has been documented, what
> is really ascertainable, what has really existed, in short, the
> whole long hieroglyphic text, so difficult to decipher, of
> humanity's moral past.　　　(GM Preface §7)

One could also note, as Leiter has done, that "modern scholars have now largely supplied the scholarly annotations that are missing, demonstrating that in writing the *Genealogy*, Nietzsche did rely extensively on contemporary scholarly literature" (Leiter 2002: 181). But, more importantly, there are good philosophical reasons to suggest that the specific way in which Williams's distinction between fictional and historical accounts is constructed in this context is itself misleading – and, indeed, unsustainable – in this context. The relevant question is whether Nietzsche's use of the literary or "fictive" device of human types entails that his genealogical accounts cannot count as truthful historical accounts, as Williams suggests. That this need not be the case becomes clear if, for example, Nietzsche's *Genealogy* stands to the history of morality as a (great) portrait stands to the subject of the painting. If this analogy holds, the fact that the *Genealogy* gives expression to the history of morality through an artistic device no more implies that it is not a truthful representation of (the character of) that history than the fact that a portrait has recourse to, say, a deliberate simplification of perspective implies that it is not a truthful representation of (the character of) the person portrayed. Indeed, the point can be put more strongly in that it may be the case that the portrait's use of a form of simplified perspective makes visible (to the relevant audience) the salient characteristics of the person portrayed in a way that is not available without the use of this artistic device. On such a view of Nietzsche's genealogy, Williams's use of the distinction between fictional and historical accounts is both misleading and unsustainable in this context. But do we have any reasons to suppose that this analogy does hold in the case of Nietzsche's *Genealogy*?

At this stage, let us consider Nietzsche's distinction (drawn in the third essay) between history (as a science) in the service of the ascetic ideal and history in the service of life. The former is characterized by the self-(mis)understanding of historical enquiry as a commitment to disinterested knowledge, to a perspectiveless grasp of the brute historical facts and to the unconditional value of historical truth in itself. In contrast, history in the service of life is characterized by an orientation around the axis of our real need, a commitment to the perspicuous interpretation of historical events and to the intrinsic (but not unconditional) value of historical truths. That Nietzsche intends the *Genealogy* to be an example of the latter can be briefly illustrated. First, in terms of the orientation of the *Genealogy* around the axis of our real need, we may merely note the following remarks from the Preface:

> Let us articulate this *new demand*: we stand in need of a *critique* of moral values, *the value of these values itself should first of all be called into question*. ... The *value* of these "values" was accepted as given, as fact, as beyond all question. Previously, no one had expressed even the remotest doubt or shown the slightest hesitation in assuming the "good man" to be of greater worth than the "evil man", of greater worth in his usefulness in promoting the progress of human *existence* (including the future of man). What? What if there existed a symptom of regression in the "good man", likewise, a danger, a temptation, a poison, a narcotic, by means of which the present were living *at the expense of the future*? Perhaps more comfortably and less dangerously, but also in less grand style, in a humbler manner? ... So that none other than morality itself would be the culprit, if the *highest power and splendour* of the human type, in itself a possibility, were never to be reached? So that morality would constitute the danger of dangers? (GM Preface §6)

Secondly, in terms of the perspicuous representation of historical events, we need simply note Nietzsche's contention in the first essay that his account makes visible a historical event – the slave revolt in morality – "which has today dropped out of sight only because it – has succeeded" (GM I §7). Nietzsche's point is that the triumph of the slave revolt in morality is expressed not least in a form of (ascetic) historiography in which the emergence of "morality" is presented not as a counter-movement to another mode of ethical reasoning but as the emergence of morality as such from a pre-moral (barbaric) context. Hence, even the "English genealogists" (i.e. Paul Rée), who represent the latest and most honest form of history in the service of the ascetic ideal, entirely obscure the event in question in virtue of their (mis)understanding of the origins of morality in terms of its present purposes, in which the character of morality is taken as read. Thirdly, in respect of the intrinsic (but not unconditional) value of historical truths, we may recall Nietzsche's gloss in *Ecce Homo*, in which he makes it clear that each essay is designed to bring forth a new truth, the value of these truths being conditional on the value of the need addressed by the *Genealogy*.

How does the fact that Nietzsche intends the *Genealogy* as an example of history in the service of life support the analogy drawn to undermine Williams's distinction between fictional and historical accounts in this context? Because history in the service of life is oriented to perspicuous representation around the axis of our real need, it operates under three constraints: first, that of being true to the object of enquiry (i.e. the history of "morality"); secondly, that of being true to the purpose of the enquiry (i.e. the re-evaluation of "morality") and, thirdly, that of being expressively adequate to its rhetorical task of persuasion. In this respect, Nietzsche's use of the dramatic device of psychological processes in human types – masters (priests and knights) and slaves – as a way of giving expression to the sociohistorical processes by which the various features that compose "morality" emerge and come to captivate us should be understood as the way of meeting the joint demands of object-salience and purpose-salience that, to Nietzsche's mind, most fully meets the further demand of expressive adequacy, that is, the reflective demand of persuasively engaging his audience. The crucial point is that this "fictive" device provides Nietzsche with a way of elucidating the ethically salient features of the history of "morality" (*ressentiment*, cruelty, partiality) that is, at once, true to that history, enables him to carry out his task of critical re-evaluation and rhetorically engages his reader's affects in the appropriate way. It is precisely because a social process involving a class of persons (e.g. slaves) can be truthfully represented as a psychological process within a singular subject-type (e.g. the slave) that Nietzsche is able to adopt this strategy.

In the light of these considerations, we can accept, *contra* Williams, the claim advanced by Nehamas, and endorsed by Geuss, that "genealogy simply *is* history correctly practiced" (Nehamas 1985: 246 n.1; cf. Geuss 1999a: 22–3), where the notion of being "correctly practised" is cashed out in terms of perspicuous representation oriented around the axis of our real need and, hence, the three constraints I have specified. We might also note that this account makes sense of Williams's reaction to the *Genealogy* as having "the property of being a once extremely compelling, in particular because it seems to hit on something with great exactitude, and at the same time of being infuriatingly vague" (Williams 2000: 157). It is compelling because it exhibits precisely the "great exactitude" that distinguishes great works of art; it appears "infuriatingly vague" to Williams because he mistakenly takes a truthful history of morality to require more in the way of historical description than Nietzsche provides. But if, as I have argued, Nietzsche's *Genealogy* does aim to give truthful expression to the history of morality, then does its critical force hang on its success in this endeavour? I think that we must conclude that while, as

Williams illustrates, this genealogy can play a critical role independent of its truth, its *full* critical force is dependent on its perspicuity and one dimension of its claim to perspicuity is the truthfulness of its representation of the history of "morality". However, judging the degree to which Nietzsche's genealogy of "morality" is perspicuous in this respect is by no means straightforward and becomes more complex still when the other dimensions of perspicuity are introduced since this requires that historical, psychological, philosophical and aesthetic considerations will all play a role in the formation of a reasonable judgement on this issue. Our entitlement to endorse or reject Nietzsche's *Genealogy* will, thus, require that we exhibit the qualities of historical spirit, psychological realism, philosophical acumen and aesthetic taste that are drawn on by Nietzsche in the composition of this work.

Conclusion

Nietzsche's *Genealogy* stands as a founding exemplar of the genealogical mode of enquiry. From the standpoint of this investigation into the character of this mode of enquiry, we can draw attention to the following features. First, the philosophical aim to which genealogy is oriented is the re-evaluation of values. Secondly, the task that genealogy confronts is (i) freeing its audience from the grip of the perspective in terms of which they currently understand their ethical agency, (ii) providing internal reasons for this audience to re-evaluate their values and (iii) doing so in a manner that is rhetorically adequate to these goals. Thirdly, it conducts this enquiry through a historical account of how we have become what we are that has recourse to the methodological stance of a non-reductive naturalism. Nietzsche is not, as he acknowledges, the first to engage in a genealogical investigation of our values but it is with his *Genealogy* that the full force of this type of investigation becomes visible.

Conclusion

No one can fail to recognize that, if true, Nietzsche's genealogies are devastating.   (Taylor 1989: 72)

At the opening of this book I drew attention to a remark by Philippa Foot: "Why do so many contemporary moral philosophers, particularly of the Anglo-American analytic school, ignore Nietzsche's attack on morality and just go on as if this extraordinary event in the history of thought had never occurred?" (1994: 3). In truth, I think that the main reason for this failure of engagement is the commitment of much, perhaps most, analytic moral philosophy to an *ahistorical* conception of their philosophical activity in which *morality* is taken as a given. The grounds for this claim are given by considering an alternative mode of moral philosophy that is *historical* in character, not in the merely instrumental sense of having an awareness of the history of moral philosophy but as seeing philosophical reflection on ethics as itself having an irreducibly historical dimension. In relation to this historical mode of philosophical reflection, Nietzsche appears as a pivotal figure, whether as a friend or as an antagonist. In this conclusion, I should like to sketch some features of this mode of *historical philosophy* as a way of reflecting on Nietzsche's own practice of philosophy and his contemporary significance.

I

It is a feature, and perhaps a distinctive one, of our modern relationship to our values that we are aware that we have inherited these values, and the concepts through which we articulate and reflect on them, as a result of a complex set of historical processes that could, in various ways, have been different. Moreover, while this history may show how our values and concepts have come to prevail, it by no means shows our outlook as necessarily having won an argument (See Williams 2006). This awareness – in so far as we acknowledge rather than avoid it[1] – has at least two significant implications. First, it poses the issue of the authority of our values as a topic for us. If we acknowledge that our inheritance of these values, and our ways of thinking about them, as authoritative is, in some part, not only a contingent matter but also one that is not vindicated by a truthful history of the process by which this inheritance came to prevail, then the legitimacy of this authority is vulnerable to reflective pressures. Such pressures may push us to address the question of the value of these values and, in doing so, to reflect on the ways in which we currently think about them. Secondly, it encourages a degree of scepticism towards forms of argument based on any straightforward appeal to our intuitions, for example our moral intuitions, since it is all too plausible that our intuitions (even relatively deep ones) may simply express the fact that we are characterized by this inheritance. Consequently, appealing to our intuitions may act as a way of deflecting, rather than acknowledging, the reflective pressures to which the authority of our values is subject.

It is, perhaps, unsurprising in the light of these considerations that one important current of work in moral and political philosophy has been concerned with reflecting on our values, and our ways of thinking about them, at least in part through recourse to historical accounts of the sources and routes through which our ethical inheritance has been composed. The basic thought that motivates this type of work is that such reflection can support or undermine confidence in our moral values and our ways of thinking about them. This basic thought can be expressed in a variety of different ways and I shall sketch five variations that have received significant contemporary expression, before returning to the case of Nietzsche's *Genealogy*.

The first variation is given in the thought that some of our ways of thinking about morality present merely the illusion of sense since the conditions of intelligibility of these ways of thinking are no longer fully present, and yet we go on as if they were. Within Anglo-American philosophy, this line of argument can be traced back to a version expressed in Elizabeth Anscombe's essay "Modern Moral Philosophy" (1981), but undoubtedly the most dramatic version of this thought in recent years has been provided by Alasdair MacIntyre's *After Virtue* (1985). In this work, MacIntyre argues "that modern moral utterance and practice can only be understood as a series of fragmented survivals from an older past and that the insoluble problems which they have generated for modern moral theorists will remain insoluble until this is well understood" (*ibid.*: 110–11). Consequently the task of understanding (and overcoming) this condition is such that only "the writing of a certain kind of history", a history that makes present the conditions of intelligibility of modern moral utterance, "will supply what we need" (*ibid.*: 113).

A second variant is presented through the thought that our mainstream ways of thinking about morality obstruct our ability to acquire a perspicuous understanding of the modern moral framework within which we are situated as moral selves. Hence we are unable to articulate our orientation to the good in such a way that the value of this orientation – and thus of our moral inheritance – becomes clear to us. The most powerful expression of this thought in recent years is provided by Charles Taylor's *Sources of the Self* (1989), which argues both that it is only through an adequate mapping of our modern moral topography that we can hope to reconcile the apparent conflicts within our moral identities and that the "articulation of modern understandings of the good has to be a historical enterprise" (*ibid.*: 103). The necessity of providing such a historical narrative, for Taylor, is not only that it is a condition of showing how we have become subject to ways of thinking about morality that leave us obscure to ourselves but also that it is precisely through such a *narrative* articulation of modern understandings of the good that we are able to orient ourselves in moral space and experience our modern moral identity as an epistemic gain (*ibid.*: 41–52).

The third example of a variation on the basic thought is the idea that our morality, and our ways of thinking about it, may be ideological (in the pejorative sense) and hence must be subject to a critical test. This variation is expressed within the tradition of critical theory that has been developed by the Frankfurt School. The nature of this variation has been summarized by Raymond Geuss as follows:

> a critical theory criticizes a set of beliefs or world-picture as ideological by showing:
> (a) that the agents in the society have a set of epistemic principles which contain a provision to the effect that beliefs which are to be sources of legitimation in the society are acceptable *only if* they could have been acquired by the agents under free and uncoerced discussion;
> (b) that the *only* reason the agents accept a particular

repressive social institution is that they think that this institution is legitimized by a set of beliefs embedded in their world-picture;

(c) that those beliefs could have been acquired by these agents *only* under conditions of coercion.

From this it follows immediately that the beliefs in question are reflectively unacceptable to the agents and that the repressive social institution these beliefs legitimize is not legitimate.   (Geuss 1981: 68)

This critical reflection on our moral beliefs is only one part of the structure of a critical theory of society but it is a crucial part in so far as the test of "reflective acceptability" serves to motivate the rational acceptance or rejection of our moral beliefs with the concomitant implications for our social institutions. The more general structure of a critical theory:

will be composed of three main constituent parts:

(A) A part which shows that a transition from the present state of society (the "initial state" of the process of emancipation) to some proposed final state is "*objectively*" or "theoretically *possible*", ...

(B) A part which shows that the transition from the present state to the proposed final state is "*practically necessary*", ...

(C) A part which asserts that the transition from the present state to the proposed final state can come about only if the agents adopt the critical theory as their "self-consciousness" and act on it.   (*Ibid.*: 76)

The test of "reflective acceptability" is the key part of B, but we should note that the role of historical reflection within such a critical theory is not simply to provide an account of the conditions under which our moral beliefs have been acquired and maintained, the legitimizing role that they play and the practical effects that they engender. It is also to show that the kind of transformation of our moral beliefs and social institutions enjoined by the critical theory is a *real*, and not simply *notional*, possibility. Indeed, it is a feature of this kind of critical theory that it argues that the historical conditions under which such a transformation is a real possibility are identical to the historical conditions under which we are capable of discerning that such a transformation is a practical necessity. In this respect, in so far as such a critical theory aims to be "the self-consciousness of a successful process of enlightenment and emancipation" (*ibid.*: 58), it is necessarily committed to the writing of a certain kind of history.

A fourth variant is provided by the *critical genealogies* composed by Michel Foucault, which consist:

> of historical studies undertaken to bring to light the two kinds of limit: to show that what is taken for granted in the form of the subject in question has a history and has been otherwise; and to show "in what has been given to us as universal, necessary and obligatory, what place is occupied by whatever is singular, contingent and the product of arbitrary constraints". These studies enable us "to free ourselves from ourselves", from this form of subjectivity, by coming to see that "that-which-is has not always been", that it could be otherwise, by showing how in Western cultures people have recognised themselves differently, and so to "alter one's way of looking at things".   (Tully 1999: 94, quoting Foucault 1984)

Starting from an inchoate sense that some feature of our subjectivity, of our ways of problematizing our experience, is a problem of the type described by the conflict between "But this isn't how it is!" and "Yet this is how it *must* be!", the kind of self-reflection that Foucault's genealogy aims to produce has the following form:

- it identifies a picture that holds us captive, whereby this captivity obstructs our capacity to make sense of ourselves as agents in ways that matter to us;
- this account involves a redescription of this picture, which contrasts it with another way of seeing the issue in order to free us from captivity to this picture;
- it provides an account of how we have become held captive by this picture, which enables us to make sense of ourselves as agents and, more particularly, to make sense of how we have failed to make sense of ourselves as agents in ways that matter to us;
- and in so far as this account engages with our cares and commitments, it motivates us to engage in the practical working out of this re-orientation of ourselves as agents.

It is in this way that genealogy performs its inherent aim to be the self-consciousness of a process of enlightenment and emancipation.

As Foucault puts it, genealogy "will separate out, from the contingency that has made us what we are, the possibility of no longer being, doing, or thinking what we are, do, or think ... seeking to give new impetus, as far and wide as possible, to the undefined work of freedom" (1997: 315–16).

A fifth variation is given in the kind of *vindicatory genealogy* undertaken by Williams in *Truth and Truthfulness* (2002), in which an initial state of nature story is given to support the claim to intrinsic value of a certain value, before it turns to focus both on the ways in which commitment to this value as an intrinsic value has been historically elaborated and deployed, and on the centrality of these elaborations and deployments to the maintenance of our contemporary ethical intelligibility. (While this fourth variant was influenced by his reading of Nietzsche in Williams's case, it owes more to Hume than Nietzsche in terms of its overall architecture.)

What is characteristic about each of these variants is that they demonstrate the possibility of *historical philosophy* as an enterprise, that is, engaging in philosophical investigation through recourse to historical enquiry (an enterprise quite distinct from either the history of philosophy or the philosophy of history or, indeed, as in Hegel, the attempted synthesis of these two enterprises). They also all locate the value of this historical mode of philosophical enquiry as fundamentally and distinctively oriented to our understanding of ourselves *qua* values. If we return to Nietzsche's *Genealogy* against this contemporary backdrop, we can situate Nietzsche's practice as a variation within this genre of historical philosophy.

Consider, first, that the initial level at which Nietzsche's *Genealogy* operates as a form of critical enquiry consists simply in providing an account of the emergence and development of our current moral outlook that is thoroughly non-vindicatory in that it shows how a variety of disparate elements have to be yoked together in a particular kind of assemblage to generate this outlook. In this respect, Nietzsche confronts us with the question of the authority of our moral outlook. However, at a second, deeper, level of critical engagement, Nietzsche's genealogy of morality aims to show that those who hold this outlook can only do so by ignoring or falsifying the historical story of how its various elements have emerged and the synthesis of these elements has developed. He does this by constructing what he takes to be a psychologically realistic and historically truthful account of this process and showing that this account cannot be accepted by those who hold the outlook in question in so far as holding this outlook requires that they have beliefs about the origins of the outlook that are incompatible with Nietzsche's account. (It is worth noting that even if one were to view Nietzsche's accounts as fictitious, they would still, in so far as they are psychologically realistic, pose a problem for the adherent of morality since the fact that, for example, an outlook that is explained by its adherents in terms of love and compassion could be equally plausibly accounted for in terms of hatred and the spirit of revenge should do rather more than merely disconcert!)

At a third and final level of critical function, Nietzsche's genealogy moves to question the intelligibility of our moral outlook by showing that it rests on presuppositions to which we can no longer be *truthfully* committed. In so far as Nietzsche's *Genealogy* is located within this mode of philosophical reflection, it is perhaps unsurprising that he is taken as a pivotal figure by the major contemporary exponents of this historical form of philosophical reflection. Thus, Nietzsche is at once a resource and opponent for the Frankfurt School (to differing degrees according to whether one is dealing with, say, Adorno or, say, Habermas), while being a crucial opponent and interlocutor for MacIntyre and Taylor and, in contrast, a guide for Foucault and Williams.

II

What, though, of any positive dimension of Nietzsche's genealogy of morality? If we consider the contemporary variants of historical philosophy, it can reasonably be argued that it is part of their critical function not simply to disorient us but also to re-orient us. The charge of nihilism that has been directed at Nietzsche's work is, I take it, most sensibly motivated by the thought that Nietzsche aims to destroy without also creating. Is there, then, any positive dimension to Nietzsche's critique of morality?

One way of responding to this question is to note that Nietzsche does indicate at least the elements of a positive ethical outlook in his critique of morality. In the first essay this is accomplished by the contrast between expressive and non-expressive accounts of human agency, on the one hand, and between the contrasting relationships to our worldly existence of the kinds of conceptions of the good endorsed by nobles and slaves. In the second essay, this work is done by the contrasting ethical outlooks of the figures of the sovereign individual and the man of bad conscience. In the final essay, this dimension is drawn out by the comparison of an outlook that treats life in instrumental terms and is oriented to the transcendence of conditions of the human existence in relation to an ethical stance that affirms our subjection to chance and necessity, to suffering and perspective, as conditions of ethical agency. While it is true that Nietzsche does not obviously integrate these elements of a positive account in the *Genealogy*, it is reasonable to see him as laying the lineaments of an ethical orientation that would be experienced by agents making the transition from "morality" as, in Taylor's phrase, an "epistemic gain" (1989: 72).

To develop a fuller account of Nietzsche's positive ethical orientation would be a rewarding and worthwhile task; it is, however, one that extends beyond the limited remit of this enquiry. For the moment, it must suffice to say that Nietzsche's critical challenge to "morality" and to modern moral philosophy remains, and awaits a compelling response.

An annotated guide to further reading

The aim of this guide is to encourage the student reader to discover more about Nietzsche by highlighting some key critical studies. Given the volume of work published on Nietzsche, I have been necessarily very selective in my choices.

Writings are divided into three sections: those that focus on the *Genealogy*; writings on Nietzsche's ethics more broadly; and some key works on Nietzsche's philosophy generally. To facilitate location, I have cited full details on any journal issue; full details on all books cited here can be found in the Bibliography.

On the *Genealogy*

Perhaps the best short, student-friendly commentary on the whole of the *Genealogy* is Chapter 4 of David Allison's *Reading the New Nietzsche* (2001), but I can also recommend the discussions in Chapter 1 of Rex Welshon's *The Philosophy of Nietzsche* (2004) and in the final chapter of R. Kevin Hill's *Nietzsche's Critiques: The Kantian Foundations of his Thought* (2003).

The best book-length studies of the *Genealogy* are Aaron Ridley's *Nietzsche's Conscience: Six Character Studies from Nietzsche's* Genealogy (1998a), Chris Janaway's *Beyond Selflessness: Reading Nietzsche's* Genealogy (2007b) and Dan Conway's *Nietzsche's* On the Genealogy of Morals: *A Reader's Guide* (2007).

Ridley's *Nietzsche's Conscience* adopts the highly illuminating strategy of focusing on the ethical-cum-psychological types (e.g. the noble, the slave, the priest) through which Nietzsche advances his argument. This works extremely well as a way of organizing and analysing Nietzsche's arguments and the result is both a rich philosophical analysis and a highly readable text. Students may also wish to look at the "Review Symposium" on this book in *Journal of Nietzsche Studies* **20** (Fall 2000). A response to Ridley's analysis of the second essay of the *Genealogy* is Matthias Risse's "The Second Treatise in *On the Genealogy of Morality*: Nietzsche on the Origin of Bad Conscience", *European Journal of Philosophy* **9** (2001), 55–81. This led to a further exchange between them on this topic in *Journal of Nietzsche Studies* **29** (Spring 2005).

Janaway's *Beyond Selflessness* starts from the standpoint of taking seriously (i) Nietzsche's acknowledgment of the relationship of the *Genealogy* to his overcoming of the influences of Schopenhauer and Rée, and (ii) the merits of a close reading that integrates Nietzsche's arguments and their rhetorical expression. Through this combination of tactics, Janaway is able to offer a highly scholarly but also very accessible reading of the *Genealogy* as a whole that is particularly illuminating on the philosophical significance of the relationship between the analytical and rhetorical dimensions of Nietzsche's text.

Conway's *Nietzsche's* On the Genealogy of Morals offers a very detailed section-by-section commentary on, and analysis of, Nietzsche's text. Although at times constrained by this structure, Conway does an excellent job of communicating the pedagogic character of the text in terms of Nietzsche's efforts to act on his readers. This, combined with Conway's own authorial stance of sympathetic yet critical analysis, allows him to track Nietzsche's arguments with considerable aplomb.

Two excellent edited collections focused on Nietzsche's *Genealogy* are Richard Schacht's *Nietzsche, Genealogy, Morality* (1994) and Christa Davis Acampora's *Nietzsche's* On the Genealogy of Morals: *Critical Essays*, which, together, contain many of the best essays published on the *Genealogy* in recent years. Schacht's volume is divided between essays addressing Nietzsche and morality and those focused on Nietzsche and genealogy; the essays by Clark, Danto, Williams, Hoy, Conway, Leiter and Schacht are particularly good. Acampora's collection moves from reflections on genealogy to interpretations of particular parts of Nietzsche's argument in the *Genealogy* to critiques of the *Genealogy* and, finally, reflections on politics and community in the *Genealogy*. Both are very worthwhile volumes, although students may find the first two parts of Acampora's collection to be more useful than Parts 3 and 4. (The essays by Ridley, Migotti and Pippin are not to be missed by any serious student.)

Some important essays and articles not contained in the above two volumes include: Raymond Geuss's "Nietzsche and Genealogy", in his *Morality, Culture and History: Essays on German Philosophy* (1999a), which notwithstanding my criticism of it in Chapter 8 of this book, is a "must read" for all students of Nietzsche; Raymond Geuss's "Nietzsche and Morality", also in *Morality, Culture, and History*, which has a superb analysis of the morality that is the target of Nietzsche's re-evaluation; Chris Janaway's "Nietzsche's Artistic Re-evalution" in *Art and Morality*, J. L. Bermudez and S. Gardner (eds) (2003), which presents a superb account of GM I §14 (that I have drawn on considerably in my own discussion); Chris Janaway's "Guilt, Bad Conscience and Self-Punishment in Nietzsche's *Genealogy*", in *Nietzsche and Morality*, B. Leiter and N. Sinhababu (eds) (2007a), which offers a highly impressive interpretation of the second essay of the *Genealogy*; Bernard Reginster's "Nietzsche on *Ressentiment* and Valuation", *Philosophy and Phenomenological Research* 57 (1997), 281–305, which makes an intriguing case for identifying the priest as the man of *ressentiment* in the *Genealogy*; Bernard Williams's "Naturalism and Genealogy", in *Morality, Reflection and Ideology*, E. Harcourt (ed.) (2000), which has much of interest to say concerning the character of genealogical enquiry.

On Nietzsche and ethics

Although not in the same class as the books noted above by Ridley and Janaway, Brian Leiter's *Nietzsche on Morality* (2002) is a very intelligent, if also very idiosyncratic, attempt to address Nietzsche as a moral philosopher and, in light of that, to offer an analysis of the *Genealogy*. Leiter's main interests concern Nietzsche's naturalism and his meta-ethics, and he has much of interest to say on these topics. Also worth mentioning in this context is another intelligent but idiosyncratic study, Randall Havas's *Nietzsche's Genealogy: Nihilism and the Will to Knowledge* (1995), which explores the issue of ethical culture in Nietzsche's work with great subtlety.

Both Leiter and Havas range wider than the *Genealogy* in addressing Nietzsche's ethics and the same is true of three books that are explicitly focused on that topic. Peter Berkowitz's *Nietzsche: The Ethics of an Immoralist* (1996) begins superbly before rather tailing off. Simon May's *Nietzsche's Ethics and his War on "Morality"* (1999) is a dense but rewarding work that illuminates many aspects of Nietzsche's concern with values and life-enhancement. A more recent contribution to the literature on Nietzsche and ethics (which unfortunately appeared too late for me to address its arguments in this book) is Bernard Reginster's excellent *The Affirmation of Life: Nietzsche on Overcoming Nihilism* (2006), which, like Janaway's *Beyond Selflessness*, is particularly strong on the relationship of Nietzsche's work to that of Schopenhauer.

On Nietzsche's philosophy

The best short guide to Nietzsche is Michael Tanner's *Nietzsche* (1994), a pithy and beautifully written introduction. Perhaps the two best general books on Nietzsche's philosophy as a whole are Richard Schacht's *Nietzsche* (1984) and Rex Welshon's *The Philosophy of Nietzsche* (2004). The Schacht volume is obviously quite old and a number of important debates have developed since it was published, but it offers much good sense and well-balanced accounts of Nietzsche's thought in terms of major philosophical themes and issues. Welshon's book is an admirably focused and crisp analysis that addresses Nietzsche's philosophy from a tough-minded analytic perspective in a refreshing and illuminating way.

Both of these books address Nietzsche on truth but it is undoubtedly Maudemarie Clark's *Nietzsche on Truth and Philosophy* (1990) that is, rightly, the locus for debates on this topic. This book is a highly sophisticated exercise in reconstructing and probing Nietzsche's philosophical development in relation to this topic that repays reading and rereading. For an intelligent response to Clark's now classic text, see R. Lanier Anderson "Overcoming Charity: The Case of Maudemarie Clark's *Nietzsche on Truth and Philosophy*", *Nietzsche-Studien* 25 (1996): 307–41 and "Nietzsche on Truth, Illusion and Redemption", *European Journal of Philosophy* 13(2) (2005), 185–225.

For more general accounts of Nietzsche's metaphysics, I can recommend two rather different books. Peter Poellner's *Nietzsche and Metaphysics* (1995) is perhaps the more traditional in that it focuses on Nietzsche's philosophy in relation to standard topics of epistemology and metaphysics. More ambitious is John Richardson's *Nietzsche's System* (1996), which attempts to articulate a coherent reading of Nietzsche's philosophy in terms of a metaphysics of will to power. Both of these books are highly intelligent studies, although a little too reliant on Nietzsche's unpublished notebooks for my taste.

Henry Staten's *Nietzsche's Voice* (1990) remains an essential work for Nietzsche scholars. Demanding and difficult, impossible to summarize, Staten's book tracks the tensions and nuances of Nietzsche's philosophical writing with a subtlety unmatched in contemporary scholarship. Tracy Strong's *Friedrich Nietzsche and the Politics of Transfiguration* (2000) was the first serious study of Nietzsche's salience for political philosophy and remains the classic work in this field. Gilles Deleuze's *Nietzsche and Philosophy* (1983) is the most important study of Nietzsche by a leading continental philosopher; highly influential on French thought and clearly written, it is an insightful and provocative work.

Useful edited collections on Nietzsche's general philosophy are Robert Solomon & Kathleen Higgins' *Reading Nietzsche* (1988), John Richardson & Brian Leiter's *Nietzsche* (2001), Richard Schacht's *Nietzsche's Postmoralism: Essays on Nietzsche's Prelude to Philosophy's Future* (2001) and Keith Ansell-Pearson's *A Companion to Nietzsche* (2005).

Notes

Introduction

1. For an effective critique of Foot's reading of Nietzsche, see M. Clark, "Nietzsche's Immoralism and the Concept of Morality", in *Nietzsche, Genealogy, Morality*, R. Schacht (ed.), 15–34 (Berkeley, CA: University of California Press, 1994). Essentially Foot fails to see that Nietzsche's immoralism is directed not at morality *per se* but at a particular ethical orientation (or what he takes to be a deformation of the ethical) that he associates with the Judeo-Christian tradition. I try to specify Nietzsche's target more fully in Chapter 4.
2. It would be hard to maintain this case since the publication of Ridley 1998a, at least in regard to the range of argument deployed.

Part I. The project of re-evaluation and the turn to genealogy

Introduction

1. Thus, for example, Leiter sees genealogy as a form of ideology critique directed to freeing "nascent higher beings from their false consciousness" about contemporary morality in which Nietzsche's voice has authority only for those predisposed to accept his values (*Nietzsche on Morality* [London: Routledge, 2002], 176 and ch. 5 more generally). Geuss, on the other hand, sees genealogy as an attempt to master Christianity by showing Christians, in terms they can accept, that the perspective composed by Nietzsche's values can give a better historical account of morality than the Christian perspective ("Nietzsche and Genealogy", in *Morality, Culture and History: Essays on German Philosophy*, 1–28 [Cambridge: Cambridge University Press, 1999a]). Similarly Ridley 1998a and S. May, *Nietzsche's Ethics and his War on "Morality"* (Oxford: Clarendon Press, 1999) see genealogy as involving a form of internal criticism that, in principle, speaks to *all* of Nietzsche's contemporaries. However, Ridley argues that "Nietzsche cannot provide a principled method for ranking competing claims to represent our most basic

interests and so must resort to a peculiar form of flattery, the kind that makes welcome even the most unpleasant revelations about ourselves provided that it also makes us feel more interesting (to us and to him)" (1998a: 152–3). It should be noted that Ridley has since rejected this view and, in "Nietzsche and the Re-evaluation of Values", *Proceedings of the Aristotelian Society* **105** (2005): 171–91, offers a nuanced account of re-evaluation that informs the argument of this essay and also provides a compelling critique of the view of re-evaluation adopted in Leiter, *Nietzsche on Morality*; see the discussion in Chapter 8 of this book.

2. On Nietzsche's relationship to Schopenhauer, see the essays in C. Janaway (ed.), *Schopenhauer as Nietzsche's Educator* (Oxford: Oxford University Press, 1998).

3. On Nietzsche's relationship to Rée, see R. Small, "Introduction", in *Paul Rée: Basic Writings*, R. Small (ed.), xi–liii (Urbana, IL: University of Illinois Press, 2003).

4. The German *Mitleid* (literally, suffering-with) can be translated as *pity* or as *compassion*. In this text, I use the two interchangeably since although Nietzsche uses the word to refer to two concepts of "suffering-with" (a noble Greek concept and an ignoble Christian concept – see D §78), these concepts do not correspond to the distinction between the concepts of pity and compassion marked out in English by these distinct words.

5. As Small notes, "The copy he [Rée] sent to Nietzsche carried the inscription 'To the father of this work most gratefully from its mother,' which Nietzsche found to be highly amusing" (Small, "Introduction", xiii).

1. Towards the project of re-evaluation

1. This essay should, as Christopher Janaway rightly says, "make us doubt whether Nietzsche ever seriously adhered to Schopenhauer's metaphysics of the will" ("Introduction", in Janway (ed.), *Schopenhauer as Nietzsche's Educator*, 1–12, esp. 19).

2. I draw this point and the distinctions between descriptive, evaluative and recommendatory aspects of pessimism from I. Soll, "Pessimism and the Tragic View of Life: Reconsiderations of Nietzsche's *Birth of Tragedy*", in *Reading Nietzsche*, R. Solomon & K. Higgins (eds), 104–31 (Oxford: Oxford University Press, 1988).

3. Nietzsche's connection with the French moralists is a significant and fascinating feature of his work that I cannot address here. For edification see R. Pippin, *Nietzsche, moraliste francais: La conception nietzscheene d'une psychologie philosophique* (Paris: Odile Jacob, 2005).

4. In endorsing this feature of Clark's essay, however, I should not be taken to also endorse her conclusions that Nietzsche remains a value anti-realist from this point on.

5. For a good discussion of this issue, see M. Clark and B. Leiter, "Introduction", in D, vii–xxxvii, esp. xv–xxiv.

6. As Clark and Leiter note, the difference in terminology can be traced to Schopenhauer's claim that what Kant calls reverence is simply obedience and, hence, that acting according to duty is acting out of fear.

7. See D §§14 and 98 for remarks on innovation in general and D §§70–72 for comments on Christianity as a successful innovation, the success of which is due, not least, to the ways in which it draws on and powerfully synthesizes a number of moral currents and beliefs already present within Jewish and Roman society.

8. Consider the distinction that Nietzsche draws between thinking and feeling in the final sentence of this passage, a distinction that refers back to his claim that our moral actions and reactions are most proximally caused by our moral sentiments rather than our moral beliefs (which stand one further step removed from our actions). This allows Nietzsche both to account for the fact that the secularization of Europe that he sees as resulting from the rise of science does not immediately lead to the collapse of Christian morality, and to register the point that whatever moral beliefs replace those of Christianity will need to become internalized as a system of moral sentiments if they are to govern our moral agency.

9. Given how frequently Nietzsche is portrayed as rejecting actions that are described in Christian morality in terms of compassion for the suffering of others, it is perhaps apposite to point out that he endorses such actions but in the Greek terms of "indignation at another's unhappiness", which he describes as "the *more manly* brother of pity" (D §78).

10. The distinction between extensional and intensional forms of suffering is borrowed from Danto (1988: 21), in which he characterizes intensional suffering as consisting in an interpretation of extensional suffering and goes on to point out – using the example of male impotence in our culture – that while one may be able to do relatively little about the extensional suffering to which those subject to impotence are exposed, it would undoubtedly reduce the overall suffering to which they are subject if sexual potence were not connected to powerful cultural images of masculinity. See in this context D §§77–8.

2. Revising the project of re-evaluation

1. By the shadows of God, Nietzsche is referring to the metaphysical analogues of God and, more generally, the deployment of our conceptual vocabulary as expressing metaphysical commitments, for example, to a particular conception of the will. See GS §127.

2. As James Conant, "Nietzsche, Kierkegaard and Anscombe on Moral Unintelligibility", in *Morality and Religion*, T. Tessin & M. von der Ruhr (eds), 250–99 (New York: St Martin's Press, 1995) and Michael Tanner, *Nietzsche* (Oxford: Oxford University Press, 1994), 33–5, have independently observed, Nietzsche's argument here bears a striking resemblance to the argument advanced by Elizabeth Anscombe (1981) in her essay "Modern Moral Philosophy", in *Ethics, Religion and Politics: Collected Philosophical Papers vol.3*, 26–42 (Oxford: Blackwell, 1981).

3. GS §357 provides a clear account with respect to philosophers of the situation recounted in GS §343.

4. Hence, within the grip of this metaphysical perspective, as Nietzsche points out in BGE, philosophers have understood their task to be that of providing

secure foundations for morality, a task that "even constitutes a type of denial that these morals *can* be regarded as a problem" (§186).

5. The meaning of the death of God will have become clear to us, on Nietzsche's account, once we recognize that "there are no viable external sources of authority", as R. Guay, "Nietzsche on Freedom", *European Journal of Philosophy* 10 (2002), 302–27, esp. 311, points out. The same point is also made by K. Gemes, "Nietzsche's Critique of Truth", *Philosophy and Phenomenological Research* 52 (1992): 47–65, esp. 50.

6. See, for example, GS §§110 and 127. B. Williams, "Nietzsche's Minimalist Moral Psychology", in *Making Sense of Humanity*, 65–76 (Cambridge: Cambridge University Press, 1995) stresses this feature of Nietzsche's approach.

7. It is a feature of the lengths to which Leiter is forced in maintaining his claim that genealogy does not involve internal criticism that he (*Nietzsche on Morality*, 175 n.7) argues that the value of truth is not internal to Christian morality although produced by it. This strikes me as a very strained reading of the textual evidence here and in GM III. Leiter is motivated to maintain this view by his commitment to the claim that Nietzsche does not want the majority to change their views, only the exceptional individuals predisposed to the values that Leiter takes Nietzsche to be espousing.

8. The contrast between Nietzsche and Hobbes is an apposite one here that has been illuminatingly explored by Paul Patton, "Nietzsche and Hobbes", *International Studies in Philosophy* 33(3) (2001), 99–116.

9. It is worth noting that Nietzsche had been edging towards the idea of will to power even when his official line focused on self-preservation. See, for example, D §§23, 112, 254 and GS §13.

10. Notably Nietzsche goes on in this passage to warn against "*superfluous* teleological principles", commenting "This is demanded by method, which must essentially be the economy of principles" (BGE §13). One of the features of Nietzsche's work that is underappreciated is his commitment to parsimony, a feature much to the fore in GM. Williams, "Nietzsche's Minimalist Moral Psychology", is one of the few to pick up on this point.

11. Note that there is nothing intentional for Nietzsche about the transformations brought about by the organic creature through the exercise of its power. Notably Nietzsche does allow that will to power can be limited to the drive to self-preservation under certain special circumstances; namely, when an organic being's relationship to its environment is such that the environment is hostile and its power to effect changes in this environment is highly restricted.

12. See M. Warren, *Nietzsche and Political Thought* (Cambridge, MA: MIT Press, 1998) for a clear exposition of this view. This construal of the doctrine of will to power avoids, it seems to me, the worries expressed by Maudemarie Clark concerning this doctrine without requiring that we adopt the rather implausible view to which she comes; namely, that the doctrine of will to power should be read "as a generalization and glorification of *the* will to power, the psychological entity (the drive or desire for power)" through which Nietzsche expresses his own "moral" values. See M. Clark, *Nietzsche on Truth and Philosophy* (Cambridge: Cambridge University Press, 1990), 224 and ch. 7 more generally. According to Clark, Nietzsche's statements concerning will to power can be divided into two very distinct classes (*ibid.*: 220–27). The

first class is composed of empirical statements concerning human psychology that can be true or false – and that present will to power as one second-order drive: the drive to experience oneself as an effective agent in the world. The second class comprises cosmological statements that are not up for grabs as true or false, and that construct an image of the world from the perspective of Nietzsche's values, that is, statements that simply (and non-mendaciously) act to glorify and generalize will to power as a second-order drive. In BGE §13, Nietzsche describes the general economy of life as will to power, a claim he repeats in GM II §12, and claims of this sort are also made in BGE §§186 and 259 and GS §349. Now, on Clark's account, we should not read these passages as empirical statements but as cosmological statements. This is because, Clark argues, Nietzsche criticizes the Stoics for projecting their moral values into nature but takes them to exemplify a general feature of philosophy:

> But this is an old and never-ending story: what formerly happened with the Stoics still happens today as soon as a philosophy begins to believe in itself. It always creates the world in its own image, it cannot do otherwise; philosophy is this tyrannical drive itself, the most spiritual will to power, to 'creation of the world', to *causa prima*. (BGE §9)

On the basis of these remarks, Clark argues:

> If he [Nietzsche] is consistent about this, he must admit that his cosmological doctrine of will to power is an attempt to read his values into the world and that he does not consider it to be true. His acceptance of it is inspired not by a will to truth, but by a will to construct the world in the image of his own values. The Stoics construct the world by picturing nature as subject to law, Nietzsche pictures the same nature as will to power. (*Nietzsche on Truth and Philosophy*, 221)

This claim hangs on assuming that Nietzsche's reference to "philosophy" in BGE §9 is intended to apply to the activity in which he is engaged – and not, say, to serve as shorthand for "metaphysical philosophy", "philosophy hitherto" or some such qualified construction. But, I suggest, we do not have any real warrant for this assumption. At a general level, we can note that the passage in question is situated in a section entitled "The Prejudices of Philosophers", which is in large part concerned with attacking metaphysical philosophy, and in a book calling for a different type of philosophy. More specifically, we can point to the sense in which BGE §9 is presented as offering a criticism of the Stoics – namely that they moralize nature – and is, thus, consonant with what is probably Nietzsche's most reiterated criticism of philosophy hitherto: that it is basically an attempt to secure some more or less local form of morality as necessarily universal (see BGE §§6 and 186, D Preface §3, etc.). But if the projection of one's values onto nature is inevitable, the critical force of the passage is limited to the notion of philosophy as advocacy proposed in BGE §5.

Nietzsche is an advocate who admits it, whereas previous philosophers have mendaciously denied that they are such (BGE §5). Such is Clark's claim, but this misses the point that Nietzsche consistently (not least throughout BGE) takes his own form of philosophical activity to be engaged in precisely the opposite procedure to that of the Stoics: not the moralization of nature but the naturalization of morality. Appealing to BGE §22, as Clark does, will not help here. Indeed, far from it being the case that "Nietzsche pretty much admits [the truth of Clark's interpretation]" (Clark, *Nietzsche on Truth and Philosophy*, 221), Nietzsche describes the moralization of nature as "bad 'philology'" and contrasts it to the good "philology" involved in his approach (BGE §22). These observations suggest that Nietzsche's point in BGE §9 is to describe what not to do (i.e. moralize nature) while acknowledging that (metaphysical) philosophy has and continues to do just this, in order to clear the way for his opposed approach: naturalizing morality. If this is cogent, the only point that remains to support Clark's view is that, on three occasions in his late works, Nietzsche's remarks have the appearance of suggesting that will to power is one drive among others (A §6, §17; TI "Expeditions of an Untimely Man" §38) but in each of these cases Nietzsche's suggestion that will to power can decline or be undermined can be accommodated by noting that the fact that agency is an expression of will to power does not entail that our capacities for agency (i.e. efficacious willing) may not be undermined by our ways of generating the feeling of power as Nietzsche's remarks on degeneration and decadence make plain. Hence I take these three remarks to refer to the undermining or decline of will to power in the sense of the undermining or decline of our powers of willing.

13. Paul Patton puts the point thus:

> Given the self-conscious, interpretative element in every human act of will, it follows that humankind is the one animal in which the feeling of power is divorced from any direct relation to quantity of power. For other higher mammals there may be a direct relationship between increase or decrease in the animal's power and the appropriate affective state: activity which enhances the animal's power leads to happiness or joy, while activity which weakens it leads to unhappiness or distress. For human beings, the link between heightened feeling of power and actual increase of power is more complex. Not only is there no necessary connection in principle, but there is a long history of magical and superstitious practices for which there is no connection in fact. This introduces the possibility that what is experienced as an increase or enhancement of power may in fact not be, while conversely what is experienced as a decrease or frustration of power may in fact be a means to its enhancement. ("Nietzsche and Hobbes", 108)

14. Note that this passage marks an important shift from *Daybreak* in that it allows Nietzsche to distinguish between the origin of a custom or way of life and its meaning; the importance of this point is stressed in GM II §12 with respect to his genealogical project.

15. Moreover, as Patton remarks:

> On the one hand, [Nietzsche] suggests that the "higher" means of attaining the feeling of power by exercising power over others are precisely those means which do not involve doing harm to others. For example, in *The Gay Science*, he states unequivocally that doing harm to others is a lesser means of producing a feeling of power in oneself than are acts of benevolence towards them: "certainly the state in which we hurt others is rarely as agreeable, in an unadulterated way, as that in which we benefit others; it is a sign that we are still lacking power, or it shows a sense of frustration in the face of this poverty ..." (GS 13). This remark implies that social relations founded upon assistance or benevolence towards others will be "more agreeable" than relations founded upon cruelty or domination.

And "more agreeable" here implies that relations of this type enhance the feeling of power to a greater degree than do relations which involve violence towards others. ... On the other hand, as the remark from *The Gay Science* 13 quoted above implies, Nietzsche views the desire to hurt others as a means of obtaining the feeling of power characteristic of those in a position of relative weakness. Rather than seeking conditions under which it can expend its own strength, the slave seeks above all to deprive others of the possibility of expending theirs. In this manner, the slave obtains its feeling of power primarily by causing harm to others, by seeking to render others incapable of action. While there is an "injustice" or cruelty towards others implicit in the situation of masters, it is not the same cruelty since it does not necessarily intend harm towards those others. The master or noble type is not by its nature committed to harming others in the manner of the slave: "The evil of the strong harms others without giving thought to it – it *has* to discharge itself; the evil of the weak *wants* to harm others and to see the signs of the suffering it has caused." (D 371).   ("Nietzsche and Hobbes", 109–10) Further support for this argument is provided by D. Owen, "Nietzsche, Enlightenment and the Problem of the Noble Ideal", in *Nietzsche's Futures*, J. Lippitt (ed.), 3–29 (Basingstoke: Macmillan, 1998), which focuses on Nietzsche's criticism of the early form of nobility identified in GM I and his concern with the prospects for a form of nobility that avoids the objectionable features that they exhibit.

16. The point that this picture is tied to a morality focused on issues of blame is nicely made in Williams, "Nietzsche's Minimalist Moral Psychology". See the later discussion of the first essay of the *Genealogy* in Chapter 5.

17. It is worth noting here that in *Beyond Good and Evil* §19, Nietzsche provides a phenomenal account of willing that demonstrates how the feeling of agency can arise from a complex set of affects that *offer* the illusion that the will is a unitary entity that stands behind, and suffices for, action. In the *Genealogy*, Nietzsche will provide an account of how and why this offer is taken up in the slave revolt in morality.

18. See D. Conway, *Nietzsche's Dangerous Game* (Cambridge: Cambridge University Press, 1997), ch. 2, for a good discussion of decadence.

19. This point is already stressed in "Schopenhauer as Educator" and it remains a prominent theme in *Daybreak* (see esp. §104). For a supportive account of the relationship between art and freedom in Nietzsche, see A. Ridley, "Art and Freedom", *European Journal of Philosophy* (2007, forthcoming) and K. Gemes, "Nietzsche on Free Will, Autonomy and the Sovereign Individual", *Proceedings of the Aristotelian Society Supp. Vol.* **80** (2006), 321–38.

20. One can think here of the early Romantics, Hegel (on some readings), Collingwood, Wittgenstein and Charles Taylor. It should be noted that this aspect of Nietzsche's thought is closely related to his inheritance, via the Romantics and Emerson, of Kant's reflections on genius; for an illuminating discussion of this point, see Conant, J. 2001. "Nietzsche's Perfectionism: A Reading of *Schopenhauer as Educator*", in *Nietzsche's Postmoralism: Essays on Nietzsche's Prelude to Philosophy's Future*, R. Schacht (ed.), 181–257 (Cambridge: Cambridge University Press, 2001), 191–6, and Ridley, "Art and Freedom".

21. Notice that it is an implication of Nietzsche's commitment to this view that the judgement that such-and-such action adequately expresses my intention is only intelligible against the background of practices in which we give and exchange reasons. What is more, I do not stand in any privileged relation to the judgement that such-and-such action adequately expresses my intention.
22. See Conant, "Nietzsche's Perfectionism", for a demonstration of this claim.
23. This view aligns Nietzsche's talk of herd-morality to his processual perfectionism. See Guay, "Nietzsche on Freedom", who calls this "meta-perfectionism" to stress the point that there is no end point or *telos* as such to Nietzsche's perfectionism, and Conant, "Nietzsche's Perfectionism", who suggests that Nietzsche's stance is akin to the Emersonian perfectionism elucidated in S. Cavell, *Conditions Handsome and Unhandsome* (Chicago, IL: University of Chicago Press, 1990). A strongly contrasting view is forthrightly argued by Leiter, *Nietzsche on Morality*. However, it is worth noting not only that Nietzsche had already criticized the elitist understanding of human excellence proposed by Leiter in "Schopenhauer as Educator", but also that Leiter's failure to address Nietzsche's concept of freedom entails that he fails to recognize that Nietzsche's remarks on herd-morality are perfectly explicable in terms that do not require the elitist understanding of human excellence to which Leiter takes Nietzsche to be committed. See Ridley, "Art and Freedom".
24. Note "self-determined" does not mean "self-imposed": the constraints may be there anyway. Rather, self-determined means affirming these constraints as conditions of one's agency. In this respect, Nietzsche's concept of freedom is closely related to his concept of fate. For a fuller discussion of this issue, see D. Owen and A. Ridley, "On Fate", *International Studies in Philosophy* 35(3) (2003), 63–78, and, in particular, the detailed critique of the argument in B. Leiter, "The Paradox of Fatalism and Self-Creation in Nietzsche", in *Schopenhauer as Nietzsche's Educator*, Janaway (ed.), 217–57, concerning Nietzsche's understanding of human types (an argument that Leiter deploys to support his claims concerning Nietzsche's commitment to the elitist view of human excellence).
25. For a powerfully developed alternative view in which perspectivism with respect to the empirical world is seen as a product of a non-perspectival metaphysics of will to power, see J. Richardson, *Nietzsche's System* (Oxford: Oxford University Press, 1996). For some scepticism – of the right kind – towards Richardson's view, see B. Reginster, "The Paradox of Perspectivism", *Philosophy and Phenomenological Research* 62 (2001), 217–33.
26. Clark (*Nietzsche on Truth and Philosophy*) is the principal figure here but other noteworthy advocates of this view include Daniel Conway, David Hoy, Brian Leiter, Bernard Reginster, Aaron Ridley and Richard Schacht, among others.
27. I think that Reginster is rather harsh in claiming that "Nietzsche is notoriously vague about what perspectives are supposed to be and he says very little about how to individuate them" ("Perspectivism, Criticism and Freedom of Spirit", *European Journal of Philosophy* 8 [2000], 40–62, esp. 43), since Nietzsche does, after all, provide plenty of examples and, with respect to the Christian perspective, much material. I think, rather, that Nietzsche's vagueness with respect to the individuation of perspectives relates, as with Wittgenstein's vagueness on the individuation of pictures, to the nature of the phenomena. Nietzsche is vague but he is vague in the right way.

28. One of the advantages of thinking about perspectives as pictures is that Wittgenstein's reflections on pictures usefully capture both the sense in which we inherit a picture (perspective) as a whole (see Wittgenstein, *On Certainty* [Oxford: Blackwell, 1975], §§140–2) and the sense that we can be held captive by a picture; it is just this condition of aspectival captivity, after all, that Nietzsche considers as obstructing his contemporaries from realizing that the death of God has significant implications for their moral commitments.

29. Note that there are two ways in which we can read Nietzsche's assertion of perspectivism. On the one hand, we may take Nietzsche to be asserting a tautology. On the other hand, we may take him to be asserting a position that risks a dilemma in which this assertion is either a performative contradiction or a claim from Nietzsche's perspective. In contrast to Reginster ("Perspectivism, Criticism and Freedom"), I incline to the former of these views.

30. This is the position that I take Reginster, "Perspectivism, Criticism and Freedom", 49–51, to argue for.

31. They might still be reasons if value *z* is an instrumental value in perspective *B* but they would not be the right sort of reasons to play the reflectively stabilizing role that they are called to play. Compare A. MacIntyre, "Dramatic Narratives, Epistemological Crises and the Philosophy of Science", *The Monist* 60 (1977), 453–72. It is one of the ironies of MacIntyre's reading of Nietzsche and, in particular, of genealogy in *Three Rival Versions of Moral Inquiry* (Notre Dame, IN: University of Notre Dame Press, 1990) that he fails to see how close Nietzsche's way of dealing with the issue of authority is to the account sketched out in his own 1977 essay.

3. Rhetorical strategies and the project of re-evaluation

1. It is a feature of Nietzsche's reflections on first and second nature that he takes the line between them to be permeable in practical terms, hence his view that our values structure our physiological constitution.

2. For an important contrasting interpretation of this passage see R. Pippin, "Nietzsche and the Melancholy of Modernity", *Social Research* 66(2) (1999), 495–519.

3. For discussion of Nietzsche's knowledge and interpretation of the work of Diogenes Laertius, see J. Barnes, "Nietzsche and Diogenes Laertius", *Nietzsche-Studien* 25 (1986), 307–41.

4. When Diogenes was reproached for eating in the marketplace, he responded, "Well, it was in the market-place that I felt hungry" (Diogenes Laertius, *Lives of the Eminent Philosophers*, vol. 2, R. D. Hicks [trans.] [Cambridge, MA: Harvard University Press, 1932], VI 56–8). This frank straightforward mode of response is, to our ears, precisely that exhibited by the madman when he points out to his audience of atheists that churches are nothing if not the tombs and sepulchres of God.

5. "When one day he was gravely discoursing and nobody attended to him, he began whistling and as people clustered about him, he reproached them with coming in all seriousness to hear nonsense, but slowly and contemptuously when the theme was serious. He would say that men strive in digging and kicking to outdo one another, but no one strives to become a good man

and true. And he would wonder that the grammarians should investigate the ills of Odysseus, while they were ignorant of their own. Or that musicians should tune the strings of the lyre, while leaving the dispositions of their souls discordant" (Laertius, *Lives of the Eminent Philosophers*, VI 26–8).

Part II. On the *Genealogy of Morality*

Introduction

1. It has recently been argued by Jacqueline Stevens, "On the Morals of Genealogy", *Political Theory* 31(4) (2003), 558–88, with some ingenuity, that Nietzsche is not advocating but, rather, criticizing the genealogical approach in the *Genealogy*. Although Stevens is right to point out that Nietzsche does criticize the English genealogists (i.e. the non-English Paul Rée) and has much of intelligence to say on this topic, she fails adequately to account for Nietzsche's stress on the "inverted and perverted" character of this kind of genealogy and mistakes the point of his reference to Rée's misreading of Darwin (a point Nietzsche stresses again in GM II §12). For these reasons, I shall retain the more straightforward account of these emphases, namely, that Nietzsche is concerned to offer an example of genealogy conducted properly.
2. On Nietzsche's relationship to Rée, and the relationship of the structure and argument of the *Genealogy* to Rée's book, see Christopher Janaway, *Beyond Selflessness: Reading Nietzsche's* Genealogy (Oxford: Oxford University Press, 2007).
3. I am grateful to Keith Ansell-Pearson for pressing me on this point, albeit that we still disagree.

4. Reading the *Genealogy*

1. For two related and overlapping characterizations of Nietzsche's target see R. Geuss, "Nietzsche and Morality", in *Morality, Culture and History: Essays on German Philosophy*, 167–97 (Cambridge: Cambridge University Press, 1999b), 171, and Leiter, *Nietzsche on Morality*, 74–81.
2. By far the best reconstruction of *On the Genealogy of Morals* as a narrative is provided by A. Ridley, *Nietzsche's Conscience: Six Character Studies from the* Genealogy (Ithaca, NY: Cornell University Press, 1998).
3. Leiter, *Nietzsche on Morality*, is a trenchant argument for this point of view; see esp. ch. 5.

5. The first essay: "'Good and Evil', 'Good and Bad'"

1. The precise target here is Paul Rée. However, as Brian Leiter notes: "It is true that, in the early 1880s, Nietzsche had been reading W. E. H. Lecky's *History of European Morals* (1869), a work which discusses authors such as the Scotsman Hume and the English philosophers Hutcheson, Bentham, and Mill, among others, all of whom were concerned in various ways with the

nature and origin of moral sentiments" (*Nietzsche on Morality*, 197–8). See also D. Thatcher, *"Zur Genealogie der Moral*: Some Textual Annotations", *Nietzsche-Studien* 18 (1989), 587–99.

2. Nietzsche's admiration of authors such as Thucydides and Machiavelli is constituted in large part by what he takes to be their commitment to psychological realism. For a brilliant exploration of the issue of Thucydides for Nietzsche, see R. Geuss, "Thucydides, Nietzsche and Williams", in his *Outside Ethics*, 219–33 (Princeton, NJ: Princeton University Press, 2005).

3. Janaway continues: "The uncanny surprise is that what initially seem opposites – the noble mode of evaluation and the slavish morality of *ressentiment* – will provoke in the reader a similar mixture of disquiet and admiration. Hence the growing unrest. The reader will find his or her own attachment to Christian or post-Christian moral values hard to stomach. Gruesome detonations occur in that the reader can be expected to suffer under the violence of this reversal in his or her affects. The new truth is among thick clouds because these freshly aroused feelings are at first hard to integrate with the rest of the reader's attitudes." ("Nietzsche's Artistic Re-evalution", in *Art and Morality*, J. L. Bermudez & S. Gardner (eds), 260–76 [London: Routledge, 2003], 262–3).

4. For support for Nietzsche's etymological claims, see M. Migotti, "Slave-morality, Socrates and the Bushmen: A Reading of the First Essay of *On the Genealogy of Morals*", *Philosophy and Phenomenological Research* 58 (1998), 745–79.

5. This is an assumption with respect to the first essay; Nietzsche provides an account of state-formation in the second essay. For the salience of the distinction between tribal and state forms of human community, see Migotti, "Slave-morality, Socrates and the Bushmen", 771–8.

6. It is this focus on typical character traits rather than other attributes such as wealth that Nietzsche is concerned with, although he notes that the nobility may also designate themselves in these others ways.

7. As we shall see in our discussion of the second essay, this claim needs to be qualified slightly in that there are circumstances in which the nobles get around this identification of agency and character through a variety of *ad hoc* devices (see GM II §23). Note that in *Beyond Good and Evil* Nietzsche stresses the point that "moral expressions everywhere first applied to *people* and then, only later and derivatively, to *actions*" (§260).

8. Note the clear implication that if this were not a situation of domination in which the slaves have no possibility of effective resistance to the rule of the nobles, the revolt would have taken a real rather than imagined form.

9. See GM II §10, in which Nietzsche notes that as communities become more powerful so they come to isolate the criminal from his act. This separation provides the basic resources needed for the thought that agents and their acts can be taken as distinct, which is, then, exploited by the slaves.

10. Note that the feeling of powerlessness that motivates the slave revolt in morality need not hang on non-recognition and, arguably, in the case of priests does not do so.

11. For some highly pertinent reflections on this section see R. Pippin, "Lightning and Flash, Agent and Deed (GM I: 6–17)", in *Friedrich Nietzsche, Genealogie der Moral*, O. Höffe (ed.), 47–63 (Berlin: Akademie Verlag, 2004), which

is especially good on Nietzsche's commitment to an expressivist account of agency.

12. Notice that Nietzsche goes on in this section to follow his rejection of (deserts) free will with an equally vehement rejection of determinism; on which point see Ridley, "Art and Freedom".

13. The claim that the priest is "the man of *ressentiment*" has been most cogently advanced by B. Reginster, "Nietzsche on *Ressentiment* and Valuation", *Philosophy and Phenomenological Research* 57 (1997), 281–305.

14. It is important to note that Nietzsche takes the slave revolt in Judaism to mark a re-evaluation of Judaic values that is prompted by the conditions of powerlessness (see A §§25–6).

15. Note that when Nietzsche talks of priests as characterized by *ressentiment*, he stresses the point that this is intrinsically related to the fact that they are characterized by the feeling of powerlessness (see GM I §7).

16. In this regard, I think that the ingenious argument of Reginster, "Nietzsche on *Ressentiment* and Valuation", goes down something of a blind alley in making the crux of Nietzsche's critical argument hang on the claim that it is the priest who initiates the slave revolt in morality.

17. It is in this respect that R. Bittner, *"Ressentiment"*, in *Nietzsche's Postmoralism*, R. Schacht (ed.), 34–46, goes wrong when attempting to sketch a paradox to the effect that either the slaves know that their revenge is imaginary, in which case it cannot compensate them, or if they do not consider it imaginary cannot have invented the values that produces the revenge. The slaves do not need to be self-consciously inventing values on Nietzsche's account; rather, it is that we must be able to see that this is what was done.

6. The second essay: "'Guilt', 'Bad Conscience' and Related Matters"

1. I draw here on the forthcoming revised Cambridge translation by Carol Diethe. The relevant German phrase in the passage cited is *"das versprechen darf"*, which has been variously translated in terms of the *right* to promise (Kaufmann/Hollingdale), being *entitled* to promise (Smith) and being *permitted* to promise (Clark/Swenson) with the last of these being perhaps the most literal translation, but Diethe's translation now strikes me as the best way of emphasizing that this is a *power* without inclining one to notions of right. I am grateful to Christa Davis Acampora for pressing me on this point, although we do not agree on its implications for the interpretation of the salience of the figure of the *sovereign individual* in Nietzsche's argument; for her view, see her "On Sovereignty and Overhumanity: Why it Matters how we Read Nietzsche *Genealogy* II: 2", *International Studies in Philosophy* 36(3) (2004), 127–45, which is also collected in her edited volume of essays on the *Genealogy: Nietzsche's* On the Genealogy of Morals: *Critical Essays* (Lanham, MD: Rowman & Littlefield, 2006).

2. These remarks preface a very interesting discussion of Nietzsche on the sovereign individual in which Lovibond (*Ethical Formation* [Cambridge, MA: Harvard University Press, 2002]) develops a compelling account of being serious in uttering certain words as part of her overall reflections on ethical formation.

3. It is notable that the ethical terms of this scale are provided by respect (in the appraisive rather than recognitive sense of this term, that is, as we might say, esteem) and contempt; terms that refer to the *character* of the agent. This is not only consistent with the form of noble morality in the first essay and, indeed, illustrates the grounds of an important remark in *Beyond Good and Evil* – "*The noble soul has reverence for itself*" (BGE §287) – but also indicates that for those who understand themselves in the light of this ethical standpoint, the failure to sustain a commitment is a source of self-contempt.

4. It should be noted that accounts – such as that endorsed by Ridley and me – of the sovereign individual as an ideal have been contested by: L. Hatab, *A Nietzschean Defence of Democracy* (Chicago, IL: Open Court, 1995); Acampora, "On Sovereignty and Overhumanity"; and P. Loeb, "Finding the *Übermensch* in Nietzsche's *Genealogy of Morality*", *Journal of Nietzsche Studies* 30 (2005), 70–101. In my view, Hatab and Acampora both make the error of confusing Nietzsche's critique of Kantian moral autonomy with a critique of ethical autonomy as such, while Loeb avoids this error only to fail to see that the figure of the sovereign individual is entirely compatible with the idea of *amor fati*.

5. I am indebted here to Chris Janaway, "Guilt, Bad Conscience, and Self-Punishment in Nietzsche's *Genealogy*", in *Nietzsche and Morality*, B. Leiter & N. Sinhababu (eds) (Oxford: Oxford University Press, 2007).

7. The third essay: "What is the Meaning of Ascetic Ideals?"

1. For a fuller discussion of the figure of the artist, see Ridley, *Nietzsche's Conscience*, ch. 4.
2. For an excellent discussion of the philosopher's relationship to the priest, see *ibid.*, ch. 3.
3. For the distinction between mythology and metaphysics, see *Daybreak* (§85) and note also *The Gay Science* (Preface §4).
4. I owe this suggestion to Chris Janaway.

8. Debating the *Genealogy*

1. Note the further acute remark that follows this point:
   It should be noted that nothing in this conception of intrinsic value entails that an intrinsic value can never, under any circumstances, be trumped by another value: in principle, any intrinsic value is capable of being trumped (depending on what other things are, and aren't, equal). It is, however, this conception of what is intrinsically valuable that, from a perspective deep within some particular way of living, may be, and often is, according to Nietzsche, mistaken for the unconditionally valuable. The facts and other values upon which an intrinsic value is conditional are so familiar, so taken for granted, as to have become invisible, and as they fade from sight so the conditionality of the intrinsic becomes invisible too.
   (Ridley, "Nietzsche and the Re-evaluation of Values", 174–5)

2. As Ridley notes:

> It may seem as if a sixth permutation is missing, namely, showing that V is indeed an intrinsic value, but is held in place by reasons and other values that are bad, although not by reasons and values that could be acknowledged as "bad" from the standpoint of the relevant way of living. This permutation, however, although formally distinct from the first kind of re-evaluation, is always likely in practice to collapse into it, since the badness of the reasons and other values holding V in place is largely going to show up via a critique of the *effects* of those reasons and values playing the role that they do in the context of some particular way of living. Given which, therefore, this form of re-evaluation slides into the re-evaluation of an intrinsic value as indirectly instrumental in realising ends which, from a perspective excluded by the way of living in question, are said to be bad, i.e., into 1. (*Ibid.*, 178)

Conclusion

1. We should note with Quentin Skinner that:

> it is remarkably difficult to avoid falling under the spell of our own intellectual heritage. As we analyse and reflect on our normative concepts, it is easy to become bewitched into believing that the ways of thinking about them bequeathed to us by the mainstream of our intellectual traditions must be *the* ways of thinking about them.
> ("Freedom and the Historian", in *Liberty before Liberalism*, 101–120 [Cambridge: Cambridge University Press, 1998], 116)

Notably Skinner goes on to suggest that:

> The intellectual historian can help us to appreciate how far the values embodied in our present way of life, and our present ways of thinking about those values, reflect a series of choices made at different times between different possible worlds. This awareness can help to liberate us from the grip of any one hegemonal account of those values and how they should be interpreted and understood. Equipped with a broader sense of possibility, we can stand back from the intellectual commitments we have inherited and ask ourselves in a new spirit of enquiry what we should think of them. (*Ibid.*: 116–17)

There is, I think, no doubting the significance of this role but we should also note that while intellectual history provides resources for addressing the question of the value of our values, and our ways of thinking about them, it does not itself (directly) take up this task.

Bibliography

Acampora, C. Davis 2004. "On Sovereignty and Overhumanity: Why it Matters how we Read Nietzsche's *Genealogy* II: 2". *International Studies in Philosophy* **36**(3): 127–45.

Acampora, C. Davis (ed.) 2006. *Nietzsche's* On the Genealogy of Morals: *Critical Essays*. Lanham, MD: Rowman & Littlefield.

Allison, D. 2001. *Reading the New Nietzsche*, Lanham, MD: Rowman & Littlefield.

Anscombe, E. 1981. "Modern Moral Philosophy". In *Ethics, Religion and Politics: Collected Philosophical Papers vol.3*, 26–42. Oxford: Blackwell.

Ansell-Pearson, K. (ed.) 2005. *A Companion to Nietzsche*. Oxford: Blackwell.

Barnes J. 1986. "Nietzsche and Diogenes Laertius". *Nietzsche-Studien* **25**: 307–41.

Berkowitz, P. 1996. *Nietzsche: The Ethics of an Immoralist*. Cambridge, MA: Harvard University Press.

Bittner, R. 2001. "*Ressentiment*". In *Nietzsche's Postmoralism: Essays on Nietzsche's Prelude to Philosophy's Future*, R. Schacht (ed.), 179–80. Oxford: Oxford University Press.

Branham, R. B. 1996. "Diogenes' Rhetoric and the *Invention* of Cynicism". In *The Cynics: The Cynic Movement in Antiquity and its Legacy*, R. B. Branham & M.-O. Goulet-Caze (eds), 81–104. Berkeley, CA: University of California Press.

Cartwright, D. 1998. "Nietzsche's Use and Abuse of Schopenhauer's Moral Philosophy for Life". See Janaway (1998a), 116–50.

Cavell, S. 1990. *Conditions Handsome and Unhandsome*. Chicago, IL: University of Chicago Press.

Clark, M. 1990. *Nietzsche on Truth and Philosophy*. Cambridge: Cambridge University Press.

Clark, M. 1994. "Nietzsche's Immoralism and the Concept of Morality". See Schacht (1994), 15–34.

Clark, M. 1998. "On Knowledge, Truth, and Value: Nietzsche's Debt to Schopenhauer and the Development of his Empiricisim". See Janaway (1998a), 37–78.

Clark, M. 2001. "On the Rejection of Morality: Bernard Williams' Debt to Nietzsche". See Schacht (2001), 100–22.

Clark, M. & B. Leiter 1997. "Introduction". In *Daybreak*, F. Nietzsche, M. Clark & B. Leiter (eds), vii–xxxvii. Cambridge: Cambridge University Press.

Conant, J. 1995. "Nietzsche, Kierkegaard and Anscombe on Moral Unintelligibility". In *Morality and Religion*, T. Tessin & M. von der Ruhr (eds), 250–99. New York: St Martin's Press.

Conant, J. 2001. "Nietzsche's Perfectionism: A Reading of *Schopenhauer as Educator*". In *Nietzsche's Postmoralism*, R. Schacht (ed.), 181–257. Cambridge: Cambridge University Press.

Conway, D. 1997. *Nietzsche's Dangerous Game*. Cambridge: Cambridge University Press.

Conway, D. 2007. *Nietzsche's* On the Genealogy of Morals: *A Reader's Guide*. London: Continuum.

Danto, A. 1988. "Some Remarks on *The Genealogy of Morals*". In *Reading Nietzsche*, R. Solomon & K. Higgins (eds), 13–28. Oxford: Oxford University Press.

Deleuze, G. 1983. *Nietzsche and Philosophy*, H. Tomlinson (trans.). London: Athlone.

Foot, P. 1994. "Nietzsche's Immoralism". See Schacht (1994), 3–14.

Foucault, M. 1984. "What is Enlightenment". In *The Foucault Reader*, P. Rabinow (ed.), 32–50. Harmondsworth: Penguin.

Foucault, M. 1997. *Ethics: The Essential Works vol. 1*, P. Rabinow (ed.). Harmondsworth: Penguin.

Frankfurt, H. 1988. *The Importance of What We Care About*. Cambridge: Cambridge University Press.

Gemes, K. 1992. "Nietzsche's Critique of Truth". *Philosophy and Phenomenological Research* 52: 47–65.

Gemes, K. 2006. "Nietzsche on Free Will, Autonomy and the Sovereign Individual". *Proceedings of the Aristotelian Society Supp. Vol.* 80: 321–38.

Geuss, R. 1981. *The Idea of a Critical Theory*. Cambridge: Cambridge University Press.

Geuss, R. 1999a. "Nietzsche and Genealogy". In *Morality, Culture and History: Essays on German Philosophy*, 1–28. Cambridge: Cambridge University Press.

Geuss, R. 1999b. "Nietzsche and Morality". In *Morality, Culture and History: Essays on German Philosophy*, 167–97. Cambridge: Cambridge University Press.

Geuss, R. 2005. "Thucydides, Nietzsche and Williams". In his *Outside Ethics*, 219–33. Princeton, NJ: Princeton University Press.

Guay, R. 2002. "Nietzsche on Freedom". *European Journal of Philosophy* 10: 302–27.

Hatab, L. 1995. *A Nietzschean Defence of Democracy*. Chicago, IL: Open Court.

Havas, R. 1995. *Nietzsche's Genealogy: Nihilism and the Will to Knowledge*. Ithaca, NY: Cornell University Press.

Heller, E. 1986. "Introduction". In *Human, All Too Human*, vol. 1, E. Heller (ed.), vii–xix. Cambridge: Cambridge University Press, 1986.

Hill, R. K. 2003. *Nietzsche's Critiques: The Kantian Foundations of his Thought*. Oxford: Clarendon Press.

Hoy, D. 1994. "Nietzsche, Hume and the Genealogical Method". See Schacht (1994), 251–68.

Kant, I. 1952. *The Critique of Judgement*, J. C. Meredith (trans.). Oxford: Oxford University Press.

Kant, I. 1991. "Idea for a Universal History with a Cosmopolitan Purpose". In *Kant's Political Writings*, H. Reiss (ed.), 41–53. Cambridge: Cambridge University Press.

Kant, I. 1996, "Groundwork of the Metaphysics of Morals". In *Practical Philosophy*, M. J. Gregor, 37–108. Cambridge: Cambridge University Press.

Janaway, C. 1988a. *Schopenhauer as Nietzsche's Educator*. Oxford: Oxford University Press.

Janaway, C. 1988b. "Introduction". See Janway (1988a), 1–12.

Janaway, C. 1988c. "Schopenhauer as Nietzsche's Educator". See Janaway (1988a), 13–36.

Janaway, C. 2003. "Nietzsche's Artistic Re-evalution". In *Art and Morality*, J. L. Bermudez & S. Gardner (eds), 260–76. London: Routledge.

Janaway, C. 2007a. "Guilt, Bad Conscience, and Self-Punishment in Nietzsche's *Genealogy*". In *Nietzsche and Morality*, B. Leiter & N. Sinhababu (eds), 138–53. Oxford: Oxford University Press.

Janaway, C. 2007b. *Beyond Selflessness: Reading Nietzsche's Genealogy*. Oxford: Oxford University Press.

Laertius, Diogenes. 1931. *Lives of the Eminent Philosophers*, vol. 2, R. D. Hicks (trans.). Cambridge, MA: Harvard University Press.

Leiter, B. 1994. "Perspectivism in Nietzsche's *Genealogy of Morals*". See Schacht (1994), 334–57.

Leiter, B. 1998. "The Paradox of Fatalism and Self-Creation in Nietzsche". See Janaway (1998a), 217–57.

Leiter, B. 2000. "Nietzsche's Metaethics: Against the Privilege Readings". *European Journal of Philosophy* 8: 277–97.

Leiter, B. 2002. *Nietzsche on Morality*. London: Routledge.

Loeb, P. 2005. "Finding the *Übermensch* in Nietzsche's *Genealogy of Morality*". *Journal of Nietzsche Studies* 30: 70–101.

Lovibond, S. 2002. *Ethical Formation*. Cambridge, MA: Harvard University Press.

MacIntyre, A. 1977. "Dramatic Narratives, Epistemological Crises and the Philosophy of Science". *The Monist* 60: 453–72.

MacIntyre, A. 1985. *After Virtue*, 2nd edn. London: Duckworth.

MacIntyre, A. 1990. *Three Rival Versions of Moral Inquiry*. Notre Dame, IN: University of Notre Dame Press.

May, S. 1999. *Nietzsche's Ethics and his War on "Morality"*. Oxford: Clarendon Press.

Migotti, M. 1998. "Slave-morality, Socrates and the Bushmen: A Reading of the First Essay of *On the Genealogy of Morals*". *Philosophy and Phenomenological Research* 58: 745–79.

Nehamas, A. 1985. *Nietzsche: Life as Literature*. Cambridge, MA: Harvard University Press.

Niehues-Pröbsting, H. 1996. "The Modern Reception Of Cynicism: Diogenes in the Enlightenment". In *The Cynics: The Cynic Movement in Antiquity and its Legacy*, R. B. Branham & M.-O. Goulet-Caze (eds), 329–65. Berkeley, CA: University of California Press.

Owen, D. 1998. "Nietzsche, Enlightenment and the Problem of the Noble Ideal". In *Nietzsche's Futures*, J. Lippitt (ed.), 3–29. Basingstoke: Macmillan.

Owen, D. & A. Ridley 2003. "On Fate". *International Studies in Philosophy* 35(3): 63–78.

Patton, P. 2001. "Nietzsche and Hobbes". *International Studies in Philosophy* 33(3): 99–116.

Pippin, R. 1999. "Nietzsche and the Melancholy of Modernity". *Social Research* 66(2): 495–519.

Pippin, R. 2004. "Lightning and Flash, Agent and Deed (GM I: 6–17)". In *Friedrich Nietzsche, Genealogie der Moral*, O. Höffe (ed.), 47–63. Berlin: Akadamie Verlag.

Pippin, R. 2005. *Nietzsche, moraliste francais: La conception nietzscheene d'une psychologie philosophique*. Paris: Odile Jacob.

Poellner, P. 1995. *Nietzsche and Metaphysics*. Oxford: Clarendon Press.

Reginster, B. 1997. "Nietzsche on *Ressentiment* and Valuation". *Philosophy and Phenomenological Research* 57: 281–305.

Reginster, B. 2000. "Perspectivism, Criticism and Freedom of Spirit". *European Journal of Philosophy* 8: 40–62.

Reginster, B. 2001. "The Paradox of Perspectivism". *Philosophy and Phenomenological Research* 62: 217–33.

Reginster, B. 2006. *The Affirmation of Life: Nietzsche on Overcoming Nihilism*. Cambridge, MA: Harvard University Press.

Richardson, J. 1996. *Nietzsche's System*. Oxford: Oxford University Press.

Richardson, J. & B. Leiter (eds) 2001. *Nietzsche*. Oxford: Oxford University Press.

Ridley, A. 1998a. *Nietzsche's Conscience: Six Character Studies from the* Genealogy. Ithaca, NY: Cornell University Press.

Ridley, A. 1998b. *Collingwood*. London: Phoenix.

Ridley, A. 2000. "Science in Service of Life". In *The Proper Ambition of Science*, M. W. F. Stone & J. Wolff (eds), 91–101. London: Routledge.

Ridley, A. 2005. "Nietzsche and the Re-evaluation of Values". *Proceedings of the Aristotelian Society* 105: 171–91.

Ridley, A. 2007a, forthcoming. "Art and Freedom". *European Journal of Philosophy*.

Ridley, A. 2007b. "Nietzsche's Intention: What the Sovereign Individual Promises". Unpublished manuscript.

Risse, M. 2001. "The Second Treatise in *On the Genealogy of Morality*: Nietzsche on the Origin of Bad Conscience". *European Journal of Philosophy* 9: 55–81.

Salaquarda, J. 1998. "Nietzsche and the Judeo-Christian Tradition". In *The Cambridge Companion to Nietzsche*, K. Higgins & B. Magnus (eds), 90–118. Cambridge: Cambridge University Press.

Schacht, R. 1984. *Nietzsche*. London: Routledge.

Schacht, R. (ed.) 1994. *Nietzsche, Genealogy, Morality*. Berkeley, CA: University of California Press.

Schacht, R. (ed.) 2001. *Nietzsche's Postmoralism: Essays on Nietzsche's Prelude to Philosophy's Future*. Cambridge: Cambridge University Press.

Skinner, Q. 1996. "Freedom and the Historian". In *Liberty before Liberalism*, 101–120. Cambridge: Cambridge University Press.

Small, R. 2003. "Introduction". In *Paul Rée: Basic Writings*, R. Small (ed.), xi–liii. Urbana, IL: University of Illinois Press.

Soll, I. 1988. "Pessimism and the Tragic View of Life: Reconsiderations of

Nietzsche's *Birth of Tragedy*". In *Reading Nietzsche*, R. Solomon & K. Higgins (eds), 104–31. Oxford: Oxford University Press.

Solomon, R. & K. Higgins (eds) 1988. *Reading Nietzsche*. Oxford: Oxford University Press.

Staten, H. 1990. *Nietzsche's Voice*. Ithaca, NY: Cornell University Press.

Stevens, J. 2003. "On the Morals of Genealogy". *Political Theory* **31**(4): 558–88.

Strong, T. 2000. *Friedrich Nietzsche and the Politics of Transfiguration*, 3rd edn. Urbana, IL: University of Illinois Press.

Tanner, M. 1994. *Nietzsche*. Oxford: Oxford University Press.

Taylor, C. 1989. *Sources of the Self*. Cambridge: Cambridge University Press.

Thatcher, D. 1989. "*Zur Genealogie der Moral*: Some Textual Annotations". *Nietzsche-Studien* **18**: 587–99.

Tully, J. 1999. "To Think and Act Differently. In *Foucault contra Habermas*, S. Ashenden & D. Owen (eds), 90–142. London: Sage.

Warren, M. 1998. *Nietzsche and Political Thought*. Cambridge, MA: MIT Press.

Welshon, R. 2004. *The Philosophy of Nietzsche*. Chesham: Acumen.

Williams, B. 1985. *Ethics and the Limits of Philosophy*. London: Fontana.

Williams, B. 1993. *Shame and Necessity*. Berkeley, CA: University of California Press.

Williams, B. 1995. "Nietzsche's Minimalist Moral Psychology". In *Making Sense of Humanity*, 65–76. Cambridge: Cambridge University Press.

Williams, B. 2000. "Naturalism and Genealogy". In *Morality, Reflection and Ideology*, E. Harcourt (ed.), 148–61. Oxford: Oxford University Press.

Williams, B. 2002. *Truth and Truthfulness*. Princeton, NJ: Princeton University Press.

Williams, B. 2006. "Philosophy as a Humanistic Discipline". In *Philosophy as a Humanistic Discipline*, A. W. Moore (ed.), 180–99. Princeton, NJ: Princeton University Press.

Wittgenstein, L. 1975. *On Certainty*. Oxford: Blackwell.

Index